Living the Life of
ENOCH

By
Ellen G. White

TEACH Services, Inc.
Brushton, New York

2006 07 08 09 10 11 12 • 5 4 3 2 1

ISBN-13: 978-1-57258-072-5
ISBN-10: 1-57258-072-0
Library of Congress Catalog Card No. 95-62230

Published by

TEACH Services, Inc.
WWW.TEACHServices.com

"Pray in your closet; and as you go about your daily labor, let your heart be often uplifted to God. It was thus that Enoch walked with God. These silent prayers rise like precious incense before the throne of grace. Satan cannot overcome him whose heart is thus stayed upon God."—*Steps to Christ, pp. 98:3–99:0.*

"We are to obey the laws of His kingdom, making ourselves all that it is possible for us to be. Earnestly we are to cultivate the highest powers of our being, remembering that we are God's property, God's building. We are required to improve every day. Even in this world of sin and sorrow, we may, by earnest, persevering effort, rise to the highest spiritual efficiency.... We are to please God. This we may do; for Enoch pleased God, though living in a degenerate age. And there are Enochs in this our day."—*Sons and Daughters, p. 314:1.*

"Enoch walked with God. So may every laborer for Christ. You may say with the psalmist, 'I have set the Lord always before me: because He is at my right hand, I shall not be moved.' Ps 16:8. While you feel that you have no sufficiency of yourself, your sufficiency will be in Jesus. If you expect all your counsel and wisdom to come from men, mortal and finite like yourselves, you will receive only human help. If you go to God for help and wisdom, He will never disappoint your faith."—*Gospel Workers (1915 ed.), pp. 417:4–418:0.*

Contents

Preface

People tell us it is too late to warn of dangers, too late to give the final message to the world, too late to expect others to respond to the pleadings of the Word of God as are presented to them.

Oh, my friends, it is not too late. We must strive and urge and plead and warn until the very day that probation ends for mankind. ***We are to live the Enoch life!***

This is our commission. And this is a twofold work—to develop a character of righteousness by living a life of personal purity and pleading with God; to teach a lesson of godliness by kindly acts and warning and pleading with men.

Enoch's example and counsels were not appreciated by many. The majority scorned and hated him. If most men merely tolerate you, then you are not living deep enough. We are not to seek their animosity, but we are not to quail before them. We are not to pick and choose and moderate our words merely that we may be accepted of all men. Come up to higher ground. The end is almost upon us. Souls are dying outside of Christ (though many think they are within). There is no time for ease for self. We must live a life of crying to Christ and pleading with men—between the mountain and the plain. Our work must not end until Jesus steps out of the Sanctuary above and human probation is finished.

And this life, properly entered into, should lead us into the country. That is God's appointed place to live in this degenerate age. It is too late for city or suburban living. "Come out of her, my people, that ye be not partakers of her sins, and that ye receive not of her plagues" (Rev 18:4). God's plan for your life is abundantly worth having. And you will find it outlined in Scripture—in the Bible and the Spirit of Prophecy.

Come, view again the life of him who is our example today,—the one who lived and walked and worked with God in an evil and corrupt time, the one who lived at the end of his time and warned the world on the verge of destruction, the one who was translated to heaven without seeing death and without having been overwhelmed by that destruction. His life is to be your life.

Come, view the life of Enoch—and you will return from the study prepared to gather warmth from the coldness of others and courage from their cowardice. You will be prepared to suffer hardship and strife and personal vilification as he did. You will be prepared to walk with God day by day, regardless of what others may say or think or do.

God bless you. I know you want to be an overcomer. God will help you day by day. His promises will never fail; open the Word of God and, with crying and strong tears, claim them. I know you want to witness for Him. He will speak through your voice, and lead you to the very ones who need your help just then. He calls you to look at the life of Enoch.

"By faith Enoch was translated that he should not see death, and was not found, because God had translated him, for before his translation he had this testimony, that he pleased God."—*Hebrews 11:5.*

Introduction

"The very atmosphere is [today] polluted with sin. Soon God's people will be tested by fiery trials, and the great proportion of those who now appear to be genuine and true will prove to be base metal. Instead of being strengthened and confirmed by opposition, threats, and abuse, they will cowardly take the side of the opposers. The promise is: 'Them that honor Me I will honor.' Shall we be less firmly attached to God's law because the world at large have attempted to make it void?

"Already the judgments of God are abroad in the land, as seen in storms, in floods, in tempests, in earthquakes, in peril by land and by sea. The great I AM is speaking to those who make void His law. When God's wrath is poured out upon the earth, who will then be able to stand? Now is the time for God's people to show themselves true to principle. When the religion of Christ is most held in contempt, when His law is most despised, then should our zeal be the warmest and our courage and firmness the most unflinching. To stand in defense of truth and righteousness when the majority forsake us, to fight the battles of the Lord when champions are few,—this will be our test. At this time we must gather warmth from the coldness of others, courage from their cowardice, and loyalty from their treason…

"The test will surely come…. The Captain of our salvation will strengthen His people for the conflict in which they must engage. How often when Satan has brought all his forces to bear against the followers of Christ, and death stares them in the face, have earnest prayers, put up in faith, brought the Captain of the Lord's host upon the field of action and turned the tide of battle and delivered the oppressed.

"Now is the time when we should closely connect with God, that we may be hid when the fierceness of His wrath is poured upon the sons of men. We have wandered away from the old landmarks. Let us return. If the Lord be God, serve Him; if Baal, serve him. Which side will you be on?"—*5 Testimonies, pp. 136:1–137:3.*

It is only as we draw near to God and study His Word and the lives of Jesus and holy men of old that we shall be strengthened to have warmth amid the coldness and apostasy around us. It was for this reason that we prepared this compilation on the life of Enoch.

"We are to obey the laws of His kingdom, making ourselves all that it is possible for us to be. Earnestly we are to cultivate the highest powers of our being, remembering that we are God's property, God's building. We are required to improve every day. Even in this world of sin and sorrow, we may, by earnest, persevering effort, rise to the highest spiritual efficiency…. We are to please God. This we may do; for Enoch pleased God, though living in a degenerate age. And there are Enochs in this our day."—*Sons and Daughters, p. 314:1.*

"I am comforted with the conviction that the Lord has made me His humble instrument in shedding some rays of precious light upon the past. Sacred History, relating to holy men of old, is brief. Inspiration has dealt sparingly in praise of the noble deeds and holy lives of the faithful. For example, the life of righteous Enoch is summed up in these words: 'And Enoch walked with God, and he was not, for God took him.' "—*Spiritual Gifts, Vol. 3, p. v:1.*

"That God who walked with Enoch was our Lord and Saviour Jesus Christ. He was the light of the world then just as He is now. Those who lived then were not without teachers to instruct them in the path of life; for Noah and Enoch were Christians. The gospel is given in precept in Leviticus. Implicit obedience is required now, as then. How essential it is that we understand the importance of this word!"—*6 Testimonies, p. 392:2.*

"The Old Testament is as verily the gospel in types and shadows as the New Testament is in its unfolding power. The New Testament does not present a new religion; the Old Testament does not present a religion to be superseded by the New. The New Testament is only the advancement and unfolding of the Old. Abel was a believer in Christ and was as verily saved by His power as was Peter or Paul. Enoch was a representative of Christ

ix

as surely as was the beloved disciple John .. That God who walked with Enoch was our Lord and Saviour, Jesus Christ. He was the light of the world then, just as He is now."—*That I May Know Him, p. 208:3.*

"This hope of redemption through the advent of the Son of God as Saviour and King, has never become extinct in the hearts of men. From the beginning there have been some whose faith has reached out beyond the shadows of the present to the realities of the future. Adam, Seth, Enoch, Methuselah, Noah, Shem, Abraham, Isaac, and Jacob—through these and other worthies the Lord has preserved the precious revealings of His will. And it was thus that to the children of Israel, the chosen people through whom was to be given to the world the promised Messiah, God imparted a knowledge of the requirements of His law, and of the salvation to be accomplished through the atoning sacrifice of His beloved Son."—*Prophets and Kings, pp. 682:2–683:0.*

"The many prophecies concerning the Saviour's advent led the Hebrews to live in an attitude of constant expectancy. Many died in the faith, not having received the promises. But having seen them afar off, they believed and confessed that they were strangers and pilgrims on the earth. From the days of Enoch the promises repeated through patriarchs and prophets had kept alive the hope of His appearing."—*Prophets and Kings, pp. 699:3–700:0.*

"How selfish was the expression that he would live a different life if he knew his Lord was to come in ten years! Why, Enoch walked with God 300 years. This is a lesson for us that we should walk with God every day, and we are not safe unless we are waiting and watching."—*Last Day Events, p. 42:5.*

"The sacrificial offerings, and the priesthood of the Jewish system, were instituted to represent the death and mediatorial work of Christ. All those ceremonies had no meaning, and no virtue, only as they related to Christ, who was Himself the foundation of, and who brought into existence, the entire system. The Lord had made known to Adam, Abel, Seth, Enoch, Noah, Abraham, and the ancient worthies, especially Moses, that the ceremonial system of sacrifices and priesthood, of themselves, were not sufficient to secure the salvation of one soul."—*Spirit of Prophecy, Vol. 2, p. 10:3.*

" 'When men shall revile you and persecute you,' said Jesus, 'rejoice, and be exceeding glad.' And He pointed His hearers to the prophets who had spoken in the name of the Lord, as 'an example of suffering affliction, and of patience.' James 5:10. Abel, the very first Christian of Adam's children, died a martyr. Enoch walked with God, and the world knew him not. Noah was mocked as a fanatic and an alarmist. 'Others had trial of cruel mockings and scourgings, yea, moreover of bonds and imprisonment.' 'Others were tortured, not accepting deliverance; that they might obtain a better resurrection.' Hebrews 11:36, 35." —*Thoughts From the Mount of Blessing*, p. 33:1.

"Yet the whole world was not corrupt. There were a few faithful witnesses for God. Methuselah, Enoch, Noah, and many others labored to keep alive on the earth the knowledge of the true God, and to stay the tide of moral evil. God declared that His Spirit should not always strive with guilty men, but that their probation should be a hundred and twenty years; if they did not then cease to pollute with their sins the world and its rich treasures, he would blot them from His creation; and these faithful ministers of righteousness gave the warning message. But the light was not heeded, and the preaching of Noah and his co-laborers impressed hearts less and less. Many, even of the worshipers of God, had not sufficient moral power to stand against the corrupting influences of the age, and were beguiled into sin by them."—*Bible Echo and Signs of the Times, July 1, 1887, para. 7.*

"In every period of this earth's history, God has had His men of opportunity, to whom He has said, 'Ye are My witnesses.' In every age there have been devout men, who gathered up the rays of light as they flashed upon their pathway, and spoke to the people the words of God. Enoch, Noah, Moses, Daniel, and the long roll of patriarchs and prophets,—these were ministers of righteousness. They were not infallible; they were weak, erring men; but the Lord wrought through them as they gave themselves to His service."—*Gospel Workers, 1915, p. 13:1.*

"Christ looked forward to the day of Pentecost, when the Holy Ghost should descend upon His disciples. He would teach them that they were not to look upon this as the result of their own labor. They were not to lose sight of the fact that patriarchs, prophets, and holy men had been sowing seeds of truth. God's ancient chosen people had been enriched with precious truth, which was to them as the river of God. Christ had been their invisible leader through all their travels in the wilderness. Gracious illustrations of His love were given them in the covenant signed by God in the rainbow of promise, which was ever to be an assurance that seedtime and harvest time should remain, and that the world should never again be destroyed by a flood. Christ was just as truly the water of life to Abel, Seth, Enoch, Noah, and all who received His instruction then, as He is at the present time to those who ask of Him the refreshing drought. God has given His Word to His chosen ones, and made known His way. Through His Son He has been supplying them with the dews and showers of His grace. But His blessings are often overlooked, and men take the glory to themselves."—*Signs of the Times, April 22, 1897, para. 17.*

"The patriarchs and prophets were representative men, and through them, from century to century, a flood of knowledge was poured into the world. Adam, repentant and converted, was a Christian; Abel was a Christian; Enoch was a Christian; Noah was a Christian; Abraham was a Christian. In types and symbols the Gospel was revealed to those of former dispensations. The Old Testament Scriptures show us the power possessed by those who looked to Christ. The glorious beams of continually increasing light are all concentrated in our time. All testify of Christ, 'the Way, the Truth, and the Life.' But never was this truth so clearly defined as in Christ's answer to the words, 'Lord, we know not whither Thou goest, and how can we know the way?' Christ is revealed to us in His first advent. We see Him sacrificing riches, power, and glory for poverty, temptation, privation, and suffering."—*Signs of the Times, January 13, 1898, para. 10.*

"In the schools established under God's direction, the fear of the Lord was the foundation of all true education. The knowledge of God had been handed down from generation to generation. In Abel, whom Cain killed, and afterward in Enoch, Seth, Methuselah, Noah, and many others, the Lord had faithful witnesses, just men, who kept His fear before their generation. Their memories were not feeble and treacherous. They had received the words of instruction from Adam, and these they repeated to their children and their children's children. Much important history and truth were expressed in song."—*Youth's Instructor, May 21, 1903, para. 8.*

"In that time, as in this, there were two classes, the righteous and the wicked. Enoch and others walked with God in uprightness. But the great majority of the inhabitants of the earth were given over to iniquity, and their wickedness rose before God. The earth 'was corrupt before God, and the earth was filled with violence.' 'The wickedness of man was great in the earth, and…every imagination of the thoughts of his heart was only evil continually.' 'And God looked upon the earth, and behold, it was corrupt; for all flesh had corrupted his way upon the earth.' 'And it repented the Lord that He had made man on the earth, and it grieved Him at His heart. And the Lord said, I will destroy man whom I have created from the face of the earth; both man and beast, and creeping things, and the fowls of the air; for it repenteth Me that I have made them.' 'And God said unto Noah, The end of all flesh is come before Me; for the earth is filled with violence through them; and, behold, I will destroy them with the earth' (Gen 6:5–13)."—*Manuscript Releases, Vol. Eighteen, pp. 92:2–93:0.*

Chapter 1
The Example of Enoch

"The experience of Enoch and of John the Baptist represents what ours should be. Far more than we do, we need to study the lives of these men,—he who was translated to heaven without seeing death; and he who, before Christ's first advent, was called to prepare the way of the Lord, to make His paths straight." —*Gospel Workers, p. 51:1.*

"Notwithstanding the prevailing iniquity, there was a line of holy men who, elevated and ennobled by communion with God, lived as in the companionship of heaven. They were men of massive intellect, of wonderful attainments. They had a great and holy mission,—to develop a character of righteousness, to teach a lesson of godliness, not only to men of their time, but for future generations. Only a few of the most prominent are mentioned in the Scriptures; but all through the ages God had faithful witnesses, truehearted worshipers.

"Of Enoch it is written that he lived sixty-five years, and begat a son. After that he walked with God three hundred years." —*Patriarchs and Prophets, p. 84:3.*

"Those who make a profession of sanctification are frequently the most proud, selfish, and overbearing. What an account will such have to render to God for their influence! They profess that their conduct is in harmony with heaven, while they manifest the evil promptings of their natural hearts. They in no way resemble Enoch, Joseph, Daniel, Paul, or Christ, the perfect Pattern. They bring Bible sanctification into contempt. Their course of conduct is uncourteous, and many times really unkind and uncouth. Such are like signboards at crossroads which mislead the traveler by pointing in the wrong direction."—*Review and Herald, September 8, 1885, para. 12.*

"Daniel and his companions were familiar with the lives of Abel, Seth, Enoch, and Noah. They cherished the truths that had been passed down from generation to generation. The image of God was engraved upon the heart. When surrounded by an atmosphere of evil, these youth remained uncorrupted. No power or influence could sway them from the principles they had learned in early life by a study of God's Word and works."—*Youth's Instructor, May 21, 1903, para. 12.*

"Enoch was a representative man, but he is not praised, he is not exalted; he simply did that which every son and daughter of Adam may do."—*Manuscript Releases, Volume Six, p. 147:1.*

"Enoch was a prophet who spake as he was moved by the Holy Ghost. He was a light amid the moral darkness, a pattern man, a man who walked with God, being obedient to God's law." —*Manuscript Releases, Volume six, p. 146:1.*

"The Bible has been your study-book. It is well thus, for it is the true counsel of God, and it is the conductor of all the holy influences that the world has contained since its creation. We have the encouraging record that Enoch walked with God. If Enoch walked with God, in that degenerate age just prior to the destruction of the world by a flood, we are to receive courage and be stimulated with his example that we need not be contaminated with the world but, amid all its corrupting influences and tendencies, we may walk with God. We may have the mind of Christ." —*Selected Messages, Book 3, p. 338:2.*

"Many regard Enoch as a man to whom God gave special power to live a life more holy than we can live. But the character of the man who was so holy that he was translated to heaven without seeing death is a representation of the character to be attained by those who will be translated when Christ comes in the clouds of heaven. Enoch's life was no more exemplary than may be the life of everyone who maintains a close connection with God."—*Signs of the Times, October 12, 1904, para. 1.*

"After Adam's fall from a state of perfect happiness to a state of misery and sin, there was danger of man's becoming discouraged, and inquiring, 'What profit is it that we have kept His ordinances and walked mournfully before the Lord,' since a heavy curse is resting upon the human race, and death is the portion of us all? But the instructions which God gave to Adam, and which were repeated by Seth, and fully exemplified by Enoch, cleared away the darkness and gloom, and gave hope to man, that as through Adam came death, through Jesus, the Promised Redeemer, would come life and immortality."—*The Spirit of Prophecy, Volume One, p. 64:1.*

"The soul who really believes the truth will carry out in his life the principles revealed in the life of Christ. Of Enoch it is written that his ways pleased God; and without faith it is impossible to please God. Not a thread of coarseness or selfishness was woven into the web that this servant of God was weaving in his daily life. And of him we read, 'Enoch walked with God...three hundred years;... and he was not; for God took him.' "—*Review and Herald, September 30, 1909, para. 4.*

Chapter 2
The Family of Enoch

"During these earlier years Enoch loved and feared God and had kept His commandments. He was one of the holy line, the preservers of the true faith, the progenitors of the promised seed. From the lips of Adam he had learned the dark story of the Fall, and the cheering one of God's grace as seen in the promise; and he relied upon the Redeemer to come. But after the birth of his first son, Enoch reached a higher experience. He was drawn into a closer relationship with God. He realized more fully his own obligations and responsibility as a son of God. And as he saw the child's love for its father, its simple trust in his protection; as he felt the deep, yearning tenderness of his own heart for that first-born son, he learned a precious lesson of the wonderful love of God to men in the gift of His Son, and the confidence which the children of God may repose in their heavenly Father. The infinite unfathomable love of God through Christ became the subject of his meditations day and night; and with all the fervor of his soul he sought to reveal that love to the people among whom he dwelt."—*Patriarchs and Prophets, p. 84:3*.

"In following Christ, looking unto Him who is the Author and Finisher of your faith, you will feel that you are working under His eye, that you are influenced by His presence, and that He knows your motives. At every step you will humbly inquire: Will this please Jesus? Will it glorify God? Morning and evening your earnest prayers should ascend to God for His blessing and guidance. True prayer takes hold upon Omnipotence and gives us the victory. Upon his knees the Christian obtains strength to resist temptation.

"The father who is the 'house band' of the family will bind his children to the throne of God by living faith. Distrusting his own strength, he hangs his helpless soul on Jesus and takes hold of the strength of the Most High. Brethren, pray at home in your family, night and morning; pray earnestly in your closet; and while engaged in your daily labor, lift up the soul to God in prayer. It was thus that Enoch walked with God. The silent, fervent prayer of the soul will rise like holy incense to the throne of grace and will be acceptable to God as if offered in the sanctuary. To all who thus seek Him, Christ becomes a present help in time of need. They will be strong in the day of trial."—*4 Testimonies, pp. 615:4–616:1.*

"There is order in heaven, and it is to be imitated by those upon earth who are heirs of salvation. The nearer mortals attain to the order and arrangement of heaven, the nearer are they brought to that acceptable state before God which will make them subjects of the heavenly kingdom and give them that fitness for translation from earth to heaven which Enoch possessed preparatory to his translation…. Brother P…has not been in harmony with that restraint, that care and diligence, which are necessary in order to preserve harmony and union of action…. A man who has but a feeble sense of his responsibility as a father to encourage and enforce order, discipline, and obedience will fail as a minister and as a shepherd of the flock. The same lack which characterizes his management at home in his family will be seen in a more public capacity in the church of God. Wrongs will exist uncorrected because of the unpleasant results which attend reproof and earnest appeal."—*2 Testimonies, pp. 697:3–698:1.*

"Enoch walked with God. He honored God in every affair of life. In his home and in his business he inquired, 'Will this be acceptable to the Lord.' And by remembering God and following His counsel, he was transformed in character, and became a godly men, whose ways pleased the Lord. We are exhorted to add to godliness, brotherly kindness. O how much we need to take this step, to add this quality to our character!… We should have that love for others that Christ has had for us. A man is estimated at his true value by the Lord of heaven. If he is unkind in his earthly home, he is unfit for the heavenly home. If he will have his own way, no matter whom it grieves, he would not be content in heaven, unless he could rule there. The love of Christ must control our hearts…. Seek God with a broken and contrite spirit, and you will be melted with compassion toward your brethren. You will

be prepared to add to brotherly kindness, charity, or love."
—*My Life Today, p. 98:3.*

"God had a church when Adam and Eve and Abel accepted and hailed with joy the good news that Jesus was their Redeemer. These realized as fully then as we realize now the promise of the presence of God in their midst. Wherever Enoch found one or two who were willing to hear the message he had for them, Jesus joined with them in their worship of God. In Enoch's day there were some among the wicked inhabitants of earth who believed. The Lord never yet has left His faithful few without His presence nor the world without a witness."—*The Upward Look, p. 228:2.*

"Enoch instructed his family in regard to the flood; Methuselah, the son of Enoch, listened to the preaching of his grandson, Noah, who faithfully warned the inhabitants of the old world that a flood of waters was coming upon the earth. Methuselah and his sons, and grandsons, lived in the time of the building of the ark. They, with some others, received instruction from Noah, and assisted him in building the ark."—*Spirit of Prophecy, Volume One, p. 65:2.*

Chapter 3
The Home of Enoch

"Enoch's walk with God was not in a trance or a vision, but in all the duties of his daily life. He did not become a hermit, shutting himself entirely from the world; for he had a work to do for God in the world. In the family and in his intercourse with men, as a husband and a father, a friend, a citizen, he was the steadfast unwavering servant of the Lord.

"His heart was in harmony with God's will; for 'can two walk together, except they be agreed?' Amos 3:3. And this holy walk was continued for three hundred years. There are few Christians who would not be far more earnest and devoted if they knew that they had but a short time to live, or that the coming of Christ was about to take place. But Enoch's faith waxed the stronger, with the lapse of centuries."—*Patriarchs and Prophets, p. 85:1–2.*

"He [Enoch] did not make his abode with the wicked. He did not locate in Sodom, thinking to save Sodom. He placed himself and his family where the atmosphere would be as pure as possible. Then at times he went forth to the inhabitants of the world with his God-given message. Every visit he made to the world was painful to him. He saw and understood something of the leprosy of sin. After proclaiming his message, he always took back with him to his place of retirement some who had received the warning. Some of these became overcomers, and died before the Flood came. But some had lived so long in the corrupting influence of sin that they could not endure righteousness."—*Manuscript 42, 1900.*

"When iniquity abounds in a nation, there is always to be heard some voice giving warning and instruction, as the voice of Lot in Sodom. Yet Lot could have preserved his family from many evils had he not made his home in this wicked, polluted city. All that Lot and his family did in Sodom [to help them] could have been done by them, even if they had lived in a place some distance away from the city. Enoch walked with God, and yet he did not live in the midst of any city polluted with every kind of violence and wickedness, as did Lot in Sodom."—*Manuscript 94, 1903.*

"If the Lord abides with us, we shall feel that we are members of Christ's family in heaven. We shall realize that angels are watching us, and our manners will be gentle and forbearing. We shall be fitting up for an entrance into the courts of heaven by cultivating courtesy and godliness…. Enoch walked with God. He honored God in every affair of life. In his home and in his business he inquired, 'Will this be acceptable to the Lord?' And by remembering God and following His counsel, he was transformed in character and became a godly man, whose ways pleased the Lord…. A man is estimated at his true value by the Lord of heaven. If he is unkind in his earthly home, he is unfit for the heavenly home. If he will have his own way, no matter whom it grieves, he would not be content in heaven, unless he could rule there. The love of Christ must control our hearts. Seek God with a broken and contrite spirit, and you will be melted with compassion toward your brethren. You will be prepared to add to brotherly kindness, charity, or love…. These steps will take us into the atmosphere of heaven."—*Review and Herald, February 21, 1888, para 11–13.*

"The cities must be worked. The millions living in these congested centers are to hear the third angel's message. This work should have been developed rapidly during the past few years. A beginning has been made, for which we praise God. Outpost centers are being established, from whence, like Enoch of old, our workers can visit the cities and do faithful service."—*Review and Herald, July 5, 1906, para 8.*

"Diligent work is now called for. In this crisis, no half-hearted efforts will prove successful. In all our city work, we are to hunt for souls. Wise plans are to be laid, in order that such work may be done to the best possible advantage. More and more, as wickedness increases in the great cities, we shall have to work them from outpost centers. This is the way Enoch labored in the days before the flood, when wickedness was rife in every populous community, and when violence was in the land."—*Review and Herald, September 27, 1906, para. 18.*

"The complete plan in regard to the purchase of the Hill Street property was not laid before me till my last visit to Los Angeles. I was then taken to see this property, and as I walked up the hill in front of it, I heard distinctly a voice that I well know. Had this voice said, 'This is the right place for God's people to purchase,' I should have been greatly astonished. But it said, 'Encourage no settlement here of any description. God forbids. My people must get away from such surroundings. This place is as Sodom for wickedness. The place where my institutions are established must be altogether different. Leave the cities, and like Enoch come from your retirement to warn the people of the cities.' "—*Manuscript Releases, Volume One, p. 250:2.*

"As God's commandment-keeping people, we must leave the cities. As did Enoch, we must work in the cities but not dwell in them."—*Evangelism, pp. 77:5–78:0.*

Chapter 4
The Prayers of Enoch

"He [Enoch] chose to be separate from them [the wicked], and spent much of his time in solitude, which he devoted to reflection and prayer. He waited before God and prayed to know His will more perfectly, that he might perform it. God communed with Enoch through His angels and gave him divine instruction. He made known to him that He would not always bear with man in his rebellion—that His purpose was to destroy the sinful race by bringing a flood of waters upon the earth."—*Story of Redemption, pp. 57:2–58:0.*

"Distressed by the increasing wickedness of the ungodly, and fearing that their infidelity might lessen his reverence for God, Enoch avoided constant association with them, and spent much time in solitude, giving himself to meditation and prayer. Thus he waited for the Lord, seeking a clearer knowledge of His will, that he might perform it. To him prayer was as the breath of the soul. He lived as in the very atmosphere of heaven."—*Patriarchs and Prophets, p. 85:4.*

"Our life is to be bound up with the life of Christ; we are to draw constantly from Him, partaking of Him, the living Bread that came down from heaven, drawing from a fountain ever fresh, ever giving forth its abundant treasures. If we keep the Lord ever before us, allowing our hearts to go out in thanksgiving and praise to Him, we shall have a continual freshness in our religious life. Our prayers will take the form of a conversation with God as we would talk with a friend. He will speak His mysteries to us personally. Often there will come to us a sweet joyful sense of the presence of Jesus. Often our hearts will burn within us as He draws nigh to commune with us as He did with Enoch. When this is in truth the experience of the Christian, there is seen in his life a simplicity, a humility, meekness, and lowliness of heart, that show to all with whom he associates that he has been with Jesus and learned of Him.

"In those who possess it, the religion of Christ will reveal itself as a vitalizing, pervading principle, a living, working, spiritual energy. There will be manifest the freshness and power and joyousness of perpetual youth. The heart that receives the Word of God is not as a pool that evaporates, not like a broken cistern that looses it treasure. It is like the mountain stream fed by unfailing springs, whose cool, sparkling waters leap from rock to rock, refreshing the weary, the thirsty, the heavy laden." —*Christ's Object Lessons, pp. 129:3–130:1.*

"I wish I could impress upon every worker in God's cause the great need of continual, earnest prayer. They cannot be constantly upon their knees, but they can be uplifting their hearts to God. This is the way that Enoch walked with God. Be careful lest self-sufficiency come in and drop Jesus out and work in your own strength rather than in the spirit and strength of the Master." —*5 Testimonies, p. 596:1.*

"Pray in your closet, and as you go about your daily labor let your heart be often uplifted to God. It was thus that Enoch walked with God. These silent prayers rise like precious incense before the throne of grace. Satan cannot overcome him whose heart is thus stayed upon God."—*Steps to Christ, pp. 98:3–99:0.*

"It is secret communion with God that sustains the soul-life... It is in the mount with God—the secret place of communion—that we are to contemplate His glorious ideal for humanity. Thus we shall be enabled so to fashion our character-building that to us may be fulfilled the promise, 'I will dwell in them, and walk in them; and I will be their God, and they shall be My people.' 2 Corinthians 6:16.

"While engaged in our daily work, we should lift the soul to heaven in prayer. These silent petitions rise like incense before the throne of grace; and the enemy is baffled. The Christian whose heart is thus stayed upon God cannot be overcome. No evil arts can destroy his peace. All the promises of God's Word, all the power of divine grace, all the resources of Jehovah are pledged to secure his deliverance. It was thus that Enoch walked with God. And God was with him, a present help in every time of need.

"Prayer is the breath of the soul. It is the secret of spiritual life. No other means of grace can be substituted, and the health of the soul be preserved.... It is only at the altar of God that we can kindle our tapers with divine fire. It is only the divine light that will reveal the littleness, the incompetence, of human ability, and give clear views of the perfection and purity of Christ. It is only as we behold Jesus that we desire to be like Him, only as we view His righteousness that we hunger and thirst to possess it; and it is only as we ask in earnest prayer, that God will grant us our heart's desire. God's messengers must tarry long with Him, if they would have success in their work."—*Gospel Workers, pp. 254:1–255:2.*

"It is only through Christ that His people can resist temptation, and become men and women of high and holy purpose, of noble integrity, who will not be swayed from truth, right, and justice. The Christian must be much in prayer. Prayer takes hold upon Omnipotence, and gains us the victory. It was thus that Enoch walked with God. And those who thus make Christ their daily companion and familiar friend will feel that the powers of an unseen world are all around them, and by looking unto Jesus they will become assimilated to His image."—*Bible Echo and Signs of the Times, October 1, 1889, para 10.*

" 'God forbid that I should glory, save in the cross of our Lord Jesus Christ, by whom the world is crucified unto me, and I unto the world.' If Christ is our personal Saviour, we shall be meditating upon His goodness and mercy and love. His presence will be with the believing, praying soul. If the believer has an intelligent knowledge of what prayer means, he will not only have stated seasons of prayer, and, after engaging in prayer at these seasons, think that his duty is done, but he will understand by experience what the Scripture means when it says, 'Enoch walked with God.' He will continually keep his mind uplifted toward God, and communion with God will give more and more desire for God, and the mind will be enlarged by contemplating the character of God. Thus he will be feeding on the flesh and blood of the son of God, who declares that He is the bread of life sent down from heaven."—*Sabbath School Worker, April 1, 1895, para. 1.*

"While engaged in our daily work, we should lift the soul to heaven in prayer. These silent petitions rise like incense before the throne of grace; and the enemy is baffled. The Christian whose heart is thus stayed upon God cannot be overcome. No evil arts can destroy his peace. All the promises of God's Word, all the power of divine grace, all the resources of Jehovah, are pledged to secure his deliverance. It was thus that Enoch walked with God. And God was with him, a present help in every time of need." —*Gospel Workers, 1915, p. 254:2.*

"Enoch walked with God. So may every laborer for Christ. You may say with the psalmist, 'I have set the Lord always before me: because He is at my right hand, I shall not be moved.' Ps 16:8. While you feel that you have no sufficiency of yourself, your sufficiency will be in Jesus. If you expect all your counsel and wisdom to come from men, mortal and finite like yourselves, you will receive only human help. If you go to God for help and wisdom, He will never disappoint your faith."—*Gospel Workers, 1915, pp. 417:4–418:0.*

"What higher power can man require than this—to be linked with the infinite God? Feeble, sinful man has the privilege of speaking to his Maker. We utter words that reach the throne of the Monarch of the universe. We pour out our heart's desire in our closets. Then we go forth to walk with God as did Enoch." —*In Heavenly Places, p. 81:6.*

"Our prayers will take the form of a conversation with God as we would talk to a friend. He will speak His mysteries to us personally. Often there will come to us a sweet joyful sense of the presence of Jesus. Often our hearts will burn within us as He draws nigh to commune with us as He did with Enoch. When this is in truth the experience of the Christian, there is seen in his life of simplicity, a humility, meekness, and lowliness of heart, that show to all with whom he associates that he has been with Jesus and learned of Him."—*Lift Him up, p. 113:7.*

Chapter 5
The Communion of Enoch

"Prayer and faith will do what no other power on earth can accomplish. We are seldom, in all respects, placed in the same position twice. We continually have new scenes and new trials to pass through, where past experience cannot be a sufficient guide. We must have the continual light that comes from God. Christ is ever sending messages to those who listen for His voice." —*Ministry of Healing, 509:2–3.*

"It is a part of God's plan to grant us, in answer to the prayer of faith, that which He would not bestow did we not thus ask." —*Great Controversy, p. 525:2.*

"We may speak with Jesus as we walk by the way, and He says, I am at thy right hand. We may commune with God in our hearts, we may walk in companionship with Christ. When engaged in our daily labor, we may breathe out our heart's desire, inaudible to any human ear; but that word cannot die away into silence, nor can it be lost. Nothing can drown the soul's desire. It rises above the din of the street, above the noise of machinery. It is God to whom we are speaking, and our prayer is heard."—*Gospel Workers, p. 258:1–2.*

"There is no time or place in which it is inappropriate to offer up a petition to God. There is nothing that can prevent us from lifting up our hearts in the spirit of earnest prayer. In the crowds of the street, in the midst of a business engagement, we may send up a petition to God, and plead for divine guidance."—*Steps to Christ, p. 98:1–99:1.*

"Every earnest petition for grace and strength will be answered .. Ask God to do for you those things that you cannot do for yourselves. Tell Jesus everything. Lay open before Him the secrets of your heart, for His eye searches the inmost recesses of the soul and He reads your thoughts as an open book. When you have asked for the things that are necessary for your soul's good, believe that you receive them, and you shall have them. Accept His gifts with your whole heart, for Jesus has died that you might have the precious things of heaven as your own, and at last find a home with the heavenly angels in the kingdom of God."—*Youth's Instructor, July 7, 1892, para. 2–4.*

"We must be much in prayer if we would make progress in the divine life. When the message of truth was first proclaimed, how much we prayed. How often was the voice of intercession heard in the chamber, in the barn, in the orchard, or the grove. Frequently we spent hours in earnest prayer, two or three together claiming the promise. Often the sound of weeping was heard and then the voice of thanksgiving and the song of praise. Now the day of God is nearer than when we first believed, and we should be more earnest, more zealous and fervent than in those early days. Our perils are greater now than then. Souls are more hardened. We need now to be imbued with the Spirit of Christ, and we should not rest until we receive it."—*5 Testimonies, pp. 161:4–162:0.*

"Cultivate the habit of talking with the Saviour.... Let the heart be continually uplifted in silent petition for help, for light, for strength, for knowledge. Let every breath be a prayer."—*Ministry of Healing, pp. 510:1–511:0.*

"The petitions of a humble heart and contrite spirit He will not despise. The opening of the hearts to our heavenly Father, the acknowledgment of our entire dependence, the expression of our wants, the homage of grateful love,—this is true prayer."—*Signs of the Times, July 1, 1886, para. 8.*

"True prayer, offered in faith, is a power to the petitioner. Prayer, whether offered in the public assembly, at the family altar, or in secret, places man directly in the presence of God. By constant prayer the youth may obtain principles so firm that the most powerful temptations will not draw them from their allegiance to God."—*Youth's Instructor, February 15, 1900, para. 1.*

"Angels record every prayer that is earnest and sincere. We should rather dispense with selfish gratifications than neglect communion with God. The deepest poverty, the greatest self-denial, with His approval, is better than riches, honors, ease, and friendship without it. We must take time to pray. If we allow our minds to be absorbed by worldly interests, the Lord may give us time by removing from us our idols of gold, of houses, or of fertile lands.... If the messengers who bear the last solemn warning to the world would pray for the blessing of God, not in a cold, listless, lazy manner, but fervently and in faith, as did Jacob, they would find many places where they could say, 'I have seen God face to face, and my life is preserved.' They would be accounted of heaven as princes, having power to prevail with God and with men."—*Great Controversy, p. 622:2–3.*

"It was by self-surrender and confiding faith that Jacob gained what he had failed to gain by conflict in his own strength. God thus taught His servant that divine power and grace alone could give him the blessing he craved. Thus it will be with those who live in the last days. As dangers surround them, and despair seizes upon the soul, they must depend solely upon the merits of the atonement. We can do nothing of ourselves. In all our helpless unworthiness we must trust in the merits of the crucified and risen Saviour. None will ever perish while they do this. The long, black catalogue of our delinquencies is before the eye of the Infinite. The register is complete; none of our offenses are forgotten. But He who listened to the cries of His servants of old, will hear the prayer of faith and pardon our transgressions. He has promised, and He will fulfill His word.

"Jacob prevailed because he was persevering and determined. His experience testifies to the power of importunate prayer. It is now that we are to learn this lesson of prevailing prayer, of unyielding faith. The greatest victories to the church of Christ or to the individual Christian are not those that are gained by talent or education, by wealth or the favor of men. They are those victories that are gained in the audience chamber with God, when earnest, agonizing faith lays hold upon the mighty arm of power."—*Patriarchs and Prophets, p. 203:0–1.*

"You need not go to the end of the earth for wisdom, for God is near.... He longs to have you reach after Him by faith. He longs to have you expect great things from Him. He longs to give you understanding in temporal as well as in spiritual matters. He can sharpen the intellect. He can give tact and skill."—*Christ's Object Lessons, p. 146:4.*

"To every one who constantly yields his will to the will of the Infinite, to be led and taught of God, there is promised an ever-increasing development of spiritual things. God fixes no limit to those who are 'filled with the knowledge of His will and in all wisdom and spiritual understanding.' "—*Review and Herald, October 4, 1906, para. 6.*

"Sometimes the Lord makes His path to the soul by a process painful to humanity. He is compelled to fortify the soul against self-esteem and self-dependence, in order that the worker shall not regard the failings and infirmities of his unsanctified nature as virtues, and thus be ruined by self-exaltation.

"If those who claim to believe the grand truths for this time would prepare themselves by searching the Scriptures, by earnest prayer and by the exercise of faith, they would place themselves where they would receive the light they so much crave…. The eloquence of silence before God is often essential. If the mind is kept in continual excitement, the ear is prevented from hearing the truth that the Lord would communicate to His believing ones. Christ takes His children from that which holds their attention, that they may behold His glory."—*Our High Calling, p. 315:4–5.*

"We will not be able to meet the trials of this time without God. We are not to have the courage and fortitude of martyrs of old until brought into the position they were in…. We are to receive daily supplies of grace for each daily emergency. Thus we grow in grace and in the knowledge of our Lord Jesus Christ, and if persecution comes upon us, if we must be enclosed in prison walls for the faith of Jesus and the keeping of God's holy law, 'As thy days, so shall thy strength be'…. The promise of God is sure, that strength shall be proportioned to our day."—*Manuscript 22, 1889.*

"The grace of Christ we cannot do without. We must have help from above if we resist the manifold temptations of Satan, and escape his devices…. Many need to learn how to pray…. When we in humility tell the Lord our wants, the Spirit itself makes intercession for us; as our sense of need causes us to lay bare our souls before the all-searching eye of Omnipotence, our earnest, fervent prayers enter within the veil, our faith claims the promises of God, and help comes to us….We must have the help which God alone can give, and that help will not come unasked…. Earnest, sincere prayer would bring strength and grace to resist the powers of darkness. God wants to bless…. But many do not feel their need. They do not realize that they can do nothing without the help of Jesus. I have been shown angels of God all ready to impart grace and power to those who feel their need of divine strength…. They have waited for the cry of souls hungering and thirsting for the blessing of God; often have they waited in vain. There were, indeed, casual prayers, but not the earnest supplication from humble, contrite hearts…. Those who would receive the blessing of the Lord, must themselves prepare the way, by confession of sin, by humiliation before God, with true penitence, and with faith in the merits of the blood of Christ." —*Manuscript 39, 1893.*

"The Life of the soul depends upon habitual communion with God. Its wants are made known, and the heart is open to receive fresh blessings. Gratitude flows from unfeigned lips; and the refreshing that is received from Jesus is manifested in words, in deeds of active benevolence, and in public devotion. There is love to Jesus in the heart; and where love exists, it will not be repressed, but will express itself. Secret prayer sustains this inner life. The heart that loves God will desire to commune with Him, and will lean on Him in holy confidence."—*Review and Herald, April 22, 1884, para. 3.*

"Seek God with all the heart. People put soul and earnestness into everything they undertake in temporal things, until their efforts are crowned with success. With intense earnestness learn the trade of seeking the rich blessings that God has promised, and with persevering, determined effort you shall have His light and His truth and His rich grace."—*Manuscript 39, 1893.*

"In sincerity, in soul hunger, cry after God. Wrestle with the heavenly agencies until you have the victory. Put your whole being into the Lord's hands—soul, body, and spirit, and resolve to be His loving, consecrated agency, moved by His will, controlled by His mind, infused with His spirit."—*Sons and Daughters of God, p. 105:5.*

"If compelled to be in the society of those who are evil, you are not compelled to enter into or engage in their evil. You can, by prayer and watching, remain unsullied by the evil manifested about you."—*Letter 16, 1867.*

" 'Commit thy way unto the Lord, trust also in Him, and He shall bring it to pass…. He shall bring forth thy righteousness as the light, and thy judgment as the noonday.' Psalm 37:5–6.

" 'The Lord also will be a refuge for the oppressed, a refuge in times of trouble. And they that know Thy name will put their trust in Thee; for Thou, Lord, has not forsaken them that seek Thee.' Psalm 9:9–10.

"The compassion that God manifests toward us, He bids us manifest toward others. Let the impulsive, the self-sufficient, the revengeful, behold the meek and lowly One, led as a lamb to the slaughter, unretaliating as a sheep dumb before her shearers. Let them look upon Him whom our sins have pierced and our sorrows burdened, and they will learn to endure, to forbear, and to forgive.

"Through faith in Christ, every deficiency of character may be supplied, every defilement cleansed, every fault corrected, every excellence developed.

" 'Ye are complete in Him.'—Colossians 2:10.

"Prayer and faith are closely allied, and they need to be studied together. In the prayer of faith there is a divine science; it is a science that every one who would make his life work a success must understand. Christ says, [1] 'What things soever ye [2] desire, when ye [3] pray, [4] believe that ye receive them, and [5] ye shall have them.' Mark 11:24. He makes plain that [1] our asking must be according to God's will; [2] we must ask for things that He has promised, and [3] whatever we receive must be used in doing His will. The conditions met, the promise is unequivocal.

"For the [1] pardon of sin, for the [2] Holy Spirit, for a [3] Christlike temper, for [4] wisdom and strength to do His work, for [5] any gift He has promised, we may [1] ask; then we are to [2] believe that we receive, and [3] return thanks to God that we have received.

"We [4] need look for no outward evidence of the blessing. The gift is in the promise, and [5] we may go about our work assured [6] that what God has promised He is able to perform, and [7] that the gift, which we already possess, [8] will be realized when we need it most.

"To live thus by the Word of God means the surrender to Him of the whole life. There will be felt a continual sense of need and dependence, a drawing out of the heart after God. Prayer is a necessity; for it is the life of the soul. Family prayer, public prayer, have their place; but it is secret communion with God that sustains the soul life.

"It was in the mount with God that Moses beheld the pattern of that wonderful building which was to be the abiding place of His glory. It is in the mount with God,—in the secret place of communion,—that we are to contemplate His glorious ideal for humanity. Thus we shall be enabled so to fashion our character building that to us may be fulfilled His promise, 'I will dwell in them, and walk in them; and I will be their God, and they shall be My people.' 2 Corinthians 6:16.

"It was in the hours of solitary prayer that Jesus in His earthly life received wisdom and power. Let the youth follow His example in finding at dawn and twilight a quiet season for communion with their Father in heaven."—*Education, pp. 257:2–259:1.*

"There are precious promises in the Scriptures to those who wait upon the Lord. We all desire an immediate answer to our prayers, and we are tempted to become discouraged if our prayer is not immediately answered. Now my experience has taught me that this is a great mistake. The delay is for our special benefit. Our faith has a chance to be tested to see whether it is true, sincere, or changeable like the waves of the sea. We must bind ourselves upon the altar with the strong cords of faith and love, and let patience have her perfect work. Faith strengthens through continual exercise."—*Letter 37, 1892.*

"We must pray more and in faith. We must not pray and then run away as though afraid we should receive an answer. God will not mock us.—He will answer if we watch unto prayer, if we believe we receive the things we ask for, and keep believing and never lose patience in believing. This is watching unto prayer. We guard the prayer of faith with expectancy and hope. We must wall it in with assurance and be not faithless, but believing. The fervent prayer of the righteous is never lost. The answer may not come according as we expected, but it will come because God's word is pledged."—*Our High Calling, p. 134:3.*

"Prayer is the breath of the soul, the channel of all blessings. As, with a realization of the needs of humanity, with a feeling of self-loathing, the repentant soul offers its prayer, God sees its struggles, watches its conflicts, and marks its sincerity. He has His finger upon its pulse, and He takes note of every throb. Not a feeling thrills it, not an emotion agitates it, not a sorrow shades it, not a sin stains it, not a thought or purpose moves it, of which He is not cognizant. That soul was purchased at an infinite cost, and is loved with a devotion that is unalterable...

"The Christian is given the invitation to carry his burdens to God in prayer, and to fasten himself closely to Christ by the cords of living faith. The Lord authorizes us to pray, declaring that He will hear the prayers of those who trust in His infinite power. He will be honored by those who draw nigh to Him, who faithfully do His service. 'Thou wilt keep him in perfect peace, whose mind is stayed on Thee, because he trusteth in thee' (Isaiah 26:3). The arm of Omnipotence is outstretched to guide us and lead us onward and still onward. Go forward, the Lord says, I understand the case, and I will send you help. Continue to pray. Have faith in Me. It is for My name's glory that you ask, and you shall receive. I will be honored before those who are watching critically for your failure. They shall see the truth triumph gloriously. 'All things, whatsoever ye ask in prayer, believing, ye shall receive.' " —*Review and Herald, October 30, 1900, para 1, 6.*

"Enoch faithfully rehearsed to the people all that had been revealed to him by the Spirit of Prophecy. Some believed his words, and turned from their wickedness to fear and worship God. Such often sought Enoch in his places of retreat, and he instructed them, and prayed for them that God would give them a knowledge of His will. He finally chose certain periods for retirement, and would not suffer the people to find him, for they interrupted his holy meditations and communion with God. He did not exclude himself at all times from the society of those who loved him and listened to his words of wisdom; neither did he separate himself wholly from the corrupt. He met with the righteous and wicked at stated times, and labored to turn the ungodly from their evil course, and instructed them in the fear of God, while he taught those who had the knowledge of God to serve Him more perfectly. He would remain with them as long as he could benefit them by his godly conversation and holy example, and then would withdraw himself for a season from all society—from the just, the scoffing idolatrous, to remain in solitude, hungering and thirsting for communion with God, and that divine knowledge which He alone could give him."—*Signs of the Times, February 20, 1879, para. 6.*

"[Enoch] was ever under the influence of Jesus. He reflected Christ's character, exhibiting the same qualities in goodness, mercy, tender compassion, sympathy, forbearance, meekness, humility, and love. His association with Christ day by day transformed him to the image of Him with whom he was so intimately connected."—*Reflecting Christ, p. 20:5.*

"By beholding, man can but admire and become more attracted to Him, more charmed and more desirous to be like Jesus until he assimilates to His image and has the mind of Christ. Like Enoch he walks with God. His mind is full of thoughts of Jesus. He is his best Friend."—*Selected Messages, Book 3, p. 169:3–170:0.*

"Communing thus with God, Enoch came more and more to reflect the divine image. His face was radiant with a holy light, even the light that shineth in the face of Jesus. As he came forth from these divine communings, even the ungodly beheld with awe the impress of heaven upon his countenance."—*Gospel Workers, 1915, p. 52:2.*

"He who is a citizen of the heavenly kingdom will be constantly looking at things not seen. The power of earth over the mind and character is broken. He has the abiding presence of the heavenly Guest, in accordance with the promise, 'I will love him, and will manifest myself to him' (John 14:21). He walks with God as did Enoch, in constant communion."—*In Heavenly Places, p. 85:1.*

"Many fail of imitating our holy Pattern because they study so little the definite features of that character. So many are full of busy plans, always active; and there is no time or place for the precious Jesus to be a close, dear Companion. They do not refer every thought and action to Him, inquiring: 'Is this the way of the Lord?' If they did they would walk with God, as did Enoch." —*Testimonies for the Church, Volume Six, p. 393:4.*

"Enoch walked with the unseen God. In the busiest places of the earth, his Companion was with him. Let all who are keeping the truth in simplicity and love, bear this in mind. The men who have the most to do have the greatest need of keeping God ever before them. When the tempter presses his suggestions upon their mind, they may, if they cherish a 'Thus saith the Lord,' be drawn into the secret pavilion of the Most High. His promises will be their safeguard. Amid all the confusion and rush of business, they will find a quiet resting place."—*This day with God, p. 232:3.*

"If thoughts of Christ, His work and character, are cherished, you will be led to sink deep the shaft of truth, and you will be enabled to come into possession of precious jewels of truth. Through an appreciation of the character of Christ, through communion with God, sin will become hateful to you. As you meditate upon heavenly things, and walk with God, as did Enoch, you will lay aside every weight and sin that doth so easily beset, and will run with patience the race set before you .. Our building must be founded upon the Rock Christ Jesus or it will not stand the test of the tempest. (*Signs of the Times, Dec. 1, 1890)*. Enoch 'walked with God'; but how did he gain this sweet intimacy? It was by having thoughts of God continually before him. As he went out and as he came in, his meditations were upon the goodness, the perfection, and the loveliness of the divine character. And as he was thus engaged, he became changed in the glorious image of his Lord; for it is by beholding that we become changed (Signs of the Times, August 18, 1887)."—*Lift Him up, p. 265:6.*

"Ministers should be instant in prayer; they should walk with God in spirit, as Enoch did of old. The divine light shining upon their countenance, and shown in their words, will illuminate the truths uttered by them, and the treasures of infinite mercy, and the Redeemer's boundless love, will be the theme of their hearts. The fervor and earnestness which characterized the work of Christ should also distinguish the efforts of His ministers. Their hearts should be subdued and filled with the Saviour's love, if they would break down the prejudice and melt the coldness of those who listen to their words. Converts seldom rise at once in spirituality above the level of their teachers. How important, then, that those teachers should habitually put their trust in God, and seek for the manifestations of His divine power upon their labors; that they should be meek, spiritual-minded, and in constant communion with Heaven. Then those who are converted under their labors will partake of their spirit, and emulate their graces."—*Review and Herald, August 8, 1878, para. 10.*

"Do not take your eyes off Jesus. Let the prayer go forth from unfeigned lips that we may not trust in our finite, human wisdom, but that our thoughts may be brought into subjection to Christ, our characters be molded after the mind of Christ. Why should we not walk with God, as did Enoch? Why should we not have the transforming grace of Christ daily? Has He not promised to us great and precious things? Who can find words to explain the rich promises of God? 'Behold,' said John, 'what manner of love the Father hath bestowed upon us, that we should be called the sons of God: therefore the world knoweth us not, because it knew Him not.' "—*Review and Herald, January 31, 1893, para. 8.*

"As Enoch of old, ministers should walk with God. The Redeemer's boundless love should be the theme of their conversation. The earnestness and unselfishness that marked the work of Christ should characterize their efforts. If they would remove prejudice from the minds of those who listen to their words, their hearts must be filled with the Saviour's love."—*Review and Herald, March 24, 1903, para. 5.*

"Christ therefore is a personal Saviour. We bear about in our body the dying of the Lord Jesus, which is life and salvation and righteousness to us. Wherever we go, we bear the abiding presence of One so dear to us; for we abide in Christ by a living faith. He is abiding in our hearts by our individual, appropriating faith. We have the companionship of the divine Jesus, and as we realize His presence, our thoughts are brought into captivity to Him. Our experience in divine things will be in proportion to the vividness of our sense of His companionship. Enoch walked with God in this way; and Christ dwells in our hearts by faith when we appreciate what He is to us, and what a work He has wrought out for us in the plan of redemption. Then we shall be most happy in cultivating a sense of this great Gift of God to our world, and to us personally."—*Signs of the Times, September 3, 1896, para. 4.*

"The soul that converses with God through the Scriptures, who prays for light and opens the door of his heart to the Saviour, will not have evil imaginings, worldly scheming, or ambitious lust after honor or distinction in any line. He who seeks for the truth as for hidden treasure will find it in God's means of communication with man, His Word. David says, 'The entrance of Thy words giveth light; it giveth understanding unto the simple.' This does not mean those who are weak in intellect, but those who, whatever their position, have a true sense of their need of conversing with God as did Enoch. The Word of God will ennoble the mind and sanctify the human agent, enabling him to become a co-worker with divine agencies. The elevated standard of God's holy law will mean very much to him, as a standard of all his life practice. It will mean holiness, which is wholeness to God. As the human agent presses forward in the path cast up for the ransomed of the Lord to walk in, as he receives Jesus Christ as his personal Saviour, he will feed on the bread of life. The Word is spirit and life, and if it is brought into the daily practice it will ennoble the whole nature of man. There will be opened to his soul such a view of the Saviour's love as portrayed by the pen of Inspiration that his heart will be melted into tenderness and contrition."—*Medical Ministry, p. 124:1.*

"It was through constant conflict and simple faith that Enoch walked with God. He realized that God is 'a very present help in trouble.' When in perplexity, he prayed to God to keep him and teach him His will. What shall I do to honor Thee, my God? was his prayer. His will was submerged in God's will. His feet were always directed in the path of obedience to God's commandments. Constantly his meditations were upon the goodness, the perfection, the loveliness, of the divine character. His conversation was upon heavenly things; he trained his mind to run in this channel. As he looked to Jesus, he became changed into the glorious image of his Lord, and his countenance was lighted up with the glory that shines from the face of Christ."—*Signs of the Times, October 12, 1904, para. 3.*

Chapter 6
The Faith of Enoch

"Thus you will obtain a most valuable experience. As you follow on to know the Lord, you will know that His goings forth are prepared as the morning. And when you receive help and comfort, sing to the praise of God. Talk with God. Thus you will become a friend of God. You will rely on Him. You will obtain a faith that will trust whether you feel like trusting or not. Remember that feeling is not an evidence that you are a Christian. Implicit faith in God shows that you are His child. Trust in God. He will never disappoint you. He says, 'I will not leave you comfortless; I will come to you. Yet a little while, and the world seeth Me no more; but ye see Me; because I live, ye shall live also.' We do not see Christ in person. It is by faith that we behold Him. Our faith grasps His promises. Thus it was that Enoch walked with God." —*Gospel Herald, March 1, 1901, para. 14.*

"It was through constant conflict and simple faith that Enoch walked with God. We may all do the same. We may be thoroughly converted and transformed, and be indeed children of God, not only enjoying His favor, but by our example, leading others in the path of humble obedience and consecration. Real godliness is diffusive and communicative. The psalmist says: 'I have not hid thy righteousness within my heart. I have declared thy faithfulness and thy salvation. I have not concealed thy loving kindness and the truth from the congregation.' This course is just the opposite of that pursued by the blind Pharisees, to whom Jesus said, 'Thy sin remaineth.' "—*Signs of the Times, June 23, 1887, para. 13.*

"As we strive to represent Christ to the world, we must exercise faith in Him. He says, 'According to your faith be it unto you.' It was by faith that Enoch walked with God. Do not ask others to exercise faith for you. You are yourself to obtain a daily experience in the things of God. You are yourself to realize the truth of the words, 'All things are possible to him that believeth.' "—*Signs of the Times, June 19, 1901, para 9.*

"He who is mighty in counsel, to whom all power in heaven and earth has been given, will come to the help of those who trust in Him. In the Scriptures we read that in certain places Christ could not do many mighty works, because of the unbelief existing there. It is of great importance that we have a faith that will not wait for the evidence of sight before it ventures to advance. 'Through faith we understand that the worlds were framed by the word of God, so that things which are seen were not made of things which do appear. By faith Abel offered unto God a more excellent sacrifice than Cain, by which he obtained witness that he was righteous, God testifying of his gifts: and by it he being dead yet speaketh. By faith Enoch was translated that he should not see death; and was not found, because God had translated him: for before his translation he had this testimony, that he pleased God. But without faith it is impossible to please Him: for he that cometh to God must believe that he is, and that he is a rewarder of them that diligently seek Him.' "—*Youth's Instructor, January 10, 1901, para. 11.*

Chapter 7
The Trust of Enoch

"He [Enoch] was of one mind with God…. If we are of one mind with God, our will will be swallowed up in God's will, and we shall follow wherever God leads the way. As a loving child places his hand in that of his father, and walks with him in perfect trust whether it is dark or bright, so the sons and daughters of God are to walk with Jesus through joy or sorrow."—*Review and Herald, December 3, 1889, para. 1.*

"You…need a through conversion to the truth, which shall slay self. Cannot you trust in God? Please read Matthew 10:25–40. Please read also, with a prayerful heart, Matthew 6:24–34. Let these words impress your heart: 'Take no thought for your life, what ye shall eat, or what ye shall drink; nor yet for your body, what ye shall put on. Is not the life more than meat, and the body than raiment?' The better life is here referred to. By the body is meant the inward adorning, which makes sinful mortals, possessing the meekness and righteousness of Christ, valuable in His sight, as was Enoch, and entitles them to receive the finishing touch of immortality. Our Saviour refers us to the fowls of the air, which sow not, neither reap, nor gather into barns, yet their heavenly Father feedeth them. Then He says, 'Are ye not much better than they?… And why take ye thought for raiment? Consider the Lilies…' These lilies, in their simplicity and innocence meet the mind of God better than Solomon in his costly decorations yet destitute of the heavenly adorning. '…Shall He not much more clothe you, O ye of little faith?' Can you not trust in your heavenly Father? 'Seek ye first the kingdom of God, and His righteousness, and all these things shall be added unto you.' Precious promise! Can we not rely upon it? Can we not have implicit trust, knowing that He is faithful who has promised? I entreat you to let your trembling faith again grasp the promises of God. Bear your whole weight upon them with unwavering faith: for they will not, they cannot, fail."—*2 Testimonies pp. 496:2–497:0.*

"If the Christian thrives and progresses at all, he must do so amid strangers to God, amid scoffing, subject to ridicule. He must stand upright like the palm tree in the desert. The sky may be as brass, the desert sand may beat about the palm tree's roots, and pile itself in heaps about its trunk. Yet the tree lives an evergreen, fresh and vigorous amid the burning desert sands. Remove the sand till you reach the rootlets of the palm tree, and you discover the secret of its life, it strikes deep beneath the surface, to the secret waters hidden in the earth. Christians indeed may be fitly represented like the palm tree. They are like Enoch; although surrounded by corrupting influences, their faith takes hold of the Unseen. They walk with God, deriving strength and grace with Him to withstand the moral pollution surrounding them…. Faith, like the rootlets of the palm tree, penetrates beneath the things which are seen, drawing spiritual nourishment from the Fountain of life."—*S.D.A. Bible Commentary, Vol. 3, p. 1151/1:4–2:0.*

"We should know what we must do to be saved. We should not, my brethren and sisters, float along with the popular current. Our present work is to come out from the world and be separate. This is the only way we can walk with God, as did Enoch. Divine influences were constantly working with his human efforts. Like Him, we are called upon to have a strong, living, working faith, and this is the only way we can be laborers together with God. We must meet the conditions laid down in the Word of God or die in our sins. We must know what moral changes are essential to be made in our characters, through the grace of Christ, in order to be fitted for the mansions above. I tell you in the fear of God: We are in danger of living like the Jews—destitute of the love of God and ignorant of His power, while the blazing light of truth is shining all around us." *5 Testimonies, pp. 535:2–536:0.*

"The Lord will work through the human agent if he will unite himself with Christ, and the record for him in the books of heaven will be, as in the case of Enoch, that he walks with God. Like Enoch, he will have a sense of God's abiding presence. The reason that so large a number of those who profess to be children of God always feel in uncertainty, is because they feel that they are orphans. They do not cultivate the precious assurance that Jesus is the sin-bearer; that although they have transgressed the law, and are sinners in His sight, yet the object of the Incarnation of Christ was to bring to the repenting, believing sinner everlasting peace and assurance. The great Advocate assumed human nature, and became like unto His brethren, to impress upon the human mind that no one who through faith accepts Him as a personal Saviour is an orphan, or is left to bear the curse of his own sins. Christians may daily cultivate faith by contemplating the One who has undertaken their cause, their 'merciful and faithful High Priest.' Having suffered, being tempted, not merely in a few things, but in all things like as we are tempted, he is able to succor all that are tempted. Even now in heaven He is afflicted in all our afflictions, and as a living Saviour he is asking intercession for us."—*Signs of the Times, November 12, 1896, para. 20.*

"How often those who trusted the Word of God, though in themselves utterly helpless, have withstood the power of the whole world: Enoch, pure in heart, holy in life, holding fast his faith in the triumph of righteousness against a corrupt and scoffing generation; Noah and his household against the men of his time, men of the greatest physical and mental strength and the most debased in morals; the children of Israel at the Red Sea, a helpless, terrified multitude of slaves, against the mightiest army of the mightiest nation on the globe; David, a shepherd lad, having God's promise of the throne, against Saul, the established monarch, bent on holding fast his power; Shadrach and his companions in the fire, and Nebuchadnezzar on the throne; Daniel among the lions, his enemies in the high places of the kingdom; Jesus on the cross, and the Jewish priests and rulers forcing even the Roman Governor to work their will; Paul in chains led to a criminal's death, Nero the despot of a world empire."—*Reflecting Christ, p. 127:2.*

"Those who would follow Christ, must believe in Him; they must open the heart to receive Him as an abiding guest. They must abide in Christ, as the branch abides in the living vine. There is a vital union formed between the parent stock and the branch, and the same fruit appears upon the branch that is seen upon the tree. Thus the Lord will work through the human agent who unites himself to Jesus Christ. Those who have an abiding trust in Christ, will, like Enoch, have a sense of the abiding presence of God. Why is it that there are so many who feel in uncertainty, who feel that they are orphans?—Is it because they do not cultivate faith in the precious assurance that the Lord Jesus is their sin-bearer. It was in behalf of those who had transgressed the law, that Jesus took upon Him human nature, and became like unto us, in order that we might have everlasting peace and assurance. We have an advocate in the heavens, and whosoever accepts Him as his personal Saviour is not left an orphan to bear the curse of his own sins."—*Sons and Daughters of God, p. 287:2.*

"When one has such a breadth of intelligence that he has outgrown his simplicity and dependence upon God, then we cannot depend on him, for Christ says, 'Without Me, ye can do nothing.' When by faith we have a right hold from above, we have an experience that we are walking with God as did Enoch. We have nothing to fear in an emergency. They that are for us are more than they that can be against us. If we are wholly consecrated to God, we shall be laborers together with Him."—*Manuscript Releases, Volume Fifteen, p. 2:1.*

Chapter 8
The Obedience of Enoch

"Let us realize the weakness of humanity, and see where man fails in his self-sufficiency. We shall then be filled with a desire to be just what God desires us to be, pure, noble, sanctified. We shall hunger and thirst after the righteousness of Christ. To be like God will be the one desire of the soul.

"This is the desire that filled Enoch's heart. And we read that he walked with God. He studied the character of God to a purpose. He did not mark out his own course, or set up his own will, as if he thought himself fully qualified to manage matters. He strove to conform himself to the divine likeness."—*Letter 169, 1903.*

"We are to obey the laws of His kingdom, making ourselves all that it is possible for us to be. Earnestly we are to cultivate the highest powers of our being, remembering that we are God's property, God's building. We are required to improve every day. Even in this world of sin and sorrow, we may by earnest, persevering effort, rise to the highest spiritual efficiency…. We are to please God. This we may do; for Enoch pleased God, though living in a degenerate age. And there are Enochs in this our day."—*Sons and Daughters of God, p. 314:2.*

"Men and women may shun the reproach they are called upon to bear for Christ's sake, they may do the works of the children of transgressors, but as surely as they do this, they will receive the reward of the evildoer. They may climb to the places of distinction, they may stand high in the literary world, and with proud superiority they may resist the truth of heavenly origin; but in the end they will lose all.

"Our happiness and salvation depend upon eating the bread of life; that is, obeying the words and doing the works of Christ, advancing righteousness and restraining unrighteousness. Nothing can give such self-reliance, such courage, such an increase of talents and ability, as a true estimate of the requirements of God's

Law.... Love for Jesus Christ leads us to obey God's commandments, which are a lamp to our feet and a light to our path, securing for us the illuminating, purifying, blissful presence of both the Father and the Son. He who is obedient can commune with God even as did Enoch."—*Sons and Daughters of God, p. 194:3–4.*

"The Lord is displeased when His people place a low estimate upon themselves. He desires His chosen heritage to value themselves according to the price He has placed upon them. God wanted them, else He would not have sent His Son on such an expensive errand to redeem them. He has a use for them, and He is well pleased when they make the very highest demands upon Him, that they may glorify His name. They may expect large things if they have faith in His promises.

"But to pray in Christ's name means much. It means that we are to accept His character, manifest His spirit, and work His works. The Saviour's promise is given on condition. 'If ye love Me,' He says, 'keep My commandments.' He saves men, not in sin, but from sin; and those who love Him will show their love by obedience.

"All true obedience comes from the heart. It was heart work with Christ. And if we consent, He will so identify Himself with our thoughts and aims, so blend our hearts and minds into conformity to His will, that when obeying Him we shall be but carrying out our own impulses. The will, refined and sanctified, will find its highest delight in doing His service. When we know God as it is our privilege to know Him, our life will be a life of continual obedience. Through an appreciation of the character of Christ, through communion with God, sin will become hateful to us.

"As Christ lived the law in humanity, so we may do if we take hold of the Strong for strength. But we are not to place the responsibility of our duty upon others, and wait for them to tell us what to do. We cannot depend for counsel upon humanity. The Lord will teach us our duty just as willingly as He will teach somebody else. If we come to Him in faith, He will speak His mysteries to us personally. Our hearts will often burn within us as One draws nigh to commune with us as He did with Enoch. Those who decide to do nothing in any line that will displease God, will know, after presenting their case before Him, just what course to pursue. And they will receive not only wisdom, but strength. Power for obedience, for service, will be imparted to them, as Christ has promised."—*Desire of Ages, p. 668:1–4.*

"God has always given men warning of coming judgments. Those who had faith in His message for their time, and who acted out their faith, in obedience to His commandments, escaped the judgments that fell upon the disobedient and unbelieving.... Because we know not the exact time of His coming, we are commanded to watch. 'Blessed are those servants, whom the Lord when He cometh shall find watching.' Luke 12:37. Those who watch for the Lord's coming are not waiting in idle expectancy. The expectation of Christ's coming is to make men fear the Lord, and fear His judgments upon transgression. It is to awaken them to the great sin of rejecting His offers of mercy. Those who are watching for the Lord are purifying their souls by obedience to the truth. With vigilant watching they combine earnest working.... They are declaring the truth that is now specially applicable. As Enoch, Noah, Abraham, and Moses each declared the truth for his time, so will Christ's servants give the special warning for their generation."—*Desire of Ages, p. 634:1–2.*

"While trusting in your heavenly Father for the help you need, He will not leave you. God has a heaven full of blessings that He wants to bestow on those who are earnestly seeking for that help which the Lord alone can give. It was in looking in faith to Jesus, in asking of Him, in believing that every word spoken would be verified, that Enoch walked with God. He kept close by the side of God, obeying His every word.... His was a wonderful life of oneness. Christ was his Companion. He was in intimate fellowship with God."—*Manuscript 111, 1898.*

"If we believe in God, we are armed with the righteousness of Christ; we have taken hold of His strength.... We want to talk with our Saviour as though He were right by our side.... It is our privilege to carry with us the credentials of our faith,—love, joy, and peace. When we do this, we shall be able to present the mighty arguments of the cross of Christ. When we learn to walk by faith and not by feeling, we shall have help from God just when we need it, and His peace will come into our hearts. It was this simple life of obedience and trust that Enoch lived. If we learn this lesson of simple trust, ours may be the testimony that he received, that he pleased God."—*My Life Today, p. 14:3–4.*

"Man is not what he might be and what it is God's will that he should be. The strong power of Satan upon the human race keeps them upon a low level; but this need not be so, else Enoch could not have become so elevated and ennobled as to walk with God. Man need not cease to grow intellectually and spiritually during his lifetime. But the minds of many are so occupied with themselves and their own selfish interests as to leave no room for higher and nobler thoughts. And the standard of intellectual as well as spiritual attainments is far too low. With many, the more responsible the position they occupy, the better pleased are they with themselves, and they cherish the idea that position gives character to the man. Few realize that they have a constant work before them to develop forbearance, sympathy, charity, conscientiousness, and fidelity."—*4 Testimonies, pp. 547:3–548:0.*

"He that is to come says, 'Behold I come quickly, and My reward is with Me to give every man according as his work shall be.' Every good deed done by the people of God as the fruit of their faith, will have its corresponding reward. As one star differeth from another star in glory, so will believers have their different spheres assigned them in the future life. Will the man who did not walk with God as did Enoch, but who walked by the side of Satan, listening to his suggestions, obeying his promptings, imperiling his own soul and the souls for whom Christ died, to gratify the carnal mind, giving lenity [mild consideration] to sin in his example—will such a man be found among the overcomers?

"When a man dies, his influence does not die with him, but it lives on reproducing itself. The influence of the man who was good and pure and holy lives on after his death, like the glow of the descending sun, casting its glories athwart the heavens, lighting up the mountain peaks long after the sun has sunk behind the hill."—*Testimonies to Ministers, pp. 428:3–429:1.*

"The dangers are many because of the unconsecrated elements that wait only until a change of circumstances shall encourage them to put all their influence on the side of wrong. If all those connected with our institutions were only devoted and spiritually minded, relying upon God more than upon themselves, there would be far greater prosperity than we have hitherto seen. But while there is such decided lack of humble trust and entire dependence upon God, we cannot be sure of anything. Our great need today is for men who are baptized with the Holy Spirit of God,—men who walk with God as did Enoch. We do not want men who are so narrow in their outlook that they will circumscribe the work instead of enlarging it, or who follow the motto: 'Religion is religion; business is business.' We need men who are farseeing, who can take in the situation and reason from cause to effect."—*5 Testimonies, p. 555:1.*

"Cultivate purity of thought, purity of life. The grace of God will be your strength to restrain your passions and curb your appetites. Earnest prayer and watching thereunto will bring the Holy Spirit to your aid to perfect the work and make you like your unerring Pattern."—*2 Testimonies, 91:2–93:0.*

"If you choose to throw off the sacred, restraining influence of the truth, Satan will lead you captive at his will. You will be in danger of giving scope to your appetites and passions, giving loose rein to lusts, to evil and abominable desires. Instead of bearing in your countenance a calm serenity under trial and affliction, like faithful Enoch, having your face radiant with hope and that peace which passeth understanding, you will stamp your countenance with carnal thoughts, with lustful desires. You will bear the impress of the satanic instead of the divine.

" 'Whereby are given unto us great and precious promises, that by these ye might be partakers of the divine nature, having escaped the corruption that is in the world through lust' (2 Peter 1:4). It is now your privilege, by humble confession and sincere repentance, to take words and return unto the Lord. The precious blood of Christ can cleanse you from all impurity, remove all your defilement, and make you perfect in Him."—*2 Testimonies, pp. 91:2–92:2.*

"Like Enoch, the physician [and you and I as well] should be a man who walks with God. This will be to him a safeguard against all the delusive, pernicious sentiments which make so many infidels and skeptics. The truth of God, practiced in the life and constantly guiding in all that concerns the interest of others, will barricade the soul with heavenly principles. God will not be unmindful of our struggle to maintain the truth. When we place every word that proceeds out of the mouth of God above worldly policy, above all the assertions of erring, failing man, we shall be guided into every good and holy way."—*Counsels to Parents and Teachers, p. 487:1.*

"In the case of Enoch, the desponding faithful were taught that, although living among a corrupt and sinful people, who were in open and daring rebellion against God, their Creator, yet if they would obey Him, and have faith in the promised Redeemer, they could work righteousness like the faithful Enoch, to be accepted of God, and finally exalted to his heavenly home."—*Spirit of Prophecy, Volume One, p. 64:2.*

"The young people of our school want to make a success of their education. Daniel made a success, when he feared God, and such a course will lead others to success; for the 'fear of the Lord is the beginning of wisdom.' You may be in a position where your influence will tell on the Lord's side. It is your exalted privilege to be a victor over the appetites and passions of the flesh, through the strength of Christ. Enoch walked with God for three hundred years. He was in harmony with the will of heaven. Enoch is a representative of the people who are to be translated from the earth. Is it not time for us to make a complete surrender to God? We must be in earnest in seeking His blessing. We must crucify the old man, with the affections and lust, in order to meet the requirements of God. Those who have been blessed of God did not cease seeking Him until they knew they had fulfilled His requirements and stood approved before Him."—*Review and Herald, March 12, 1889, para. 3.*

"God has purchased us by the death of His Son. He desires us to remember that we are His, and that by the right use of our endowments we are to make of ourselves all that it is possible for us to be. Earnestly we are to cultivate the highest powers of our being, striving by persevering effort to rise to the highest spiritual efficiency. In spirit, in word, in action, we are to please God. This we may do; for Enoch pleased God, though living in an degenerate age. The power at Enoch's command is also at our command."—*Signs of the Times, July 24, 1901, para. 2.*

"The spirit which Enoch, Joseph, and Daniel possessed, we may have. We may draw from the same source of strength, and realize the same power of self-control; and the same graces may shine out in our lives."—*Our High Calling, p. 278:6.*

"Our happiness and salvation depend upon eating the bread of life; that is, obeying the words and doing the works of Christ, advancing righteousness and restraining unrighteousness. Nothing can give such self-reliance, such courage, such an increase of talents and ability, as a true estimate of the requirements of God's law…. Love for Jesus Christ leads us to obey God's commandments, which are a lamp to our feet and a light to our path, securing for us the illuminating, purifying, blissful presence of both the Father and the Son. He who is obedient can commune with God even as did Enoch."—*Sons and Daughters of God, p. 194:4.*

"How few are aware that they have darling idols, that they have cherished sins! God sees these sins to which you may be blinded, and He works with His pruning knife to strike deep and separate these cherished sins from you. You all want to choose for yourselves the process of purification. How hard it is for you to submit to the crucifixion of self; but when the work is all submitted to God, to Him who knows our weakness and our sinfulness, He takes the very best way to bring about the desired results. It was through constant conflict and simple faith that Enoch walked with God. You may all do the same. You may be thoroughly converted and transformed, and be indeed children of God, enjoying not only the knowledge of His will, but, by your example, leading others in the same path of humble obedience and consecration. Real godliness is diffusive and communicative. The psalmist says: 'I have hid Thy righteousness within my heart; I have declared Thy faithfulness and Thy salvation: I have not concealed Thy loving-kindness and Thy truth from the great congregation.' Wherever the love of God is, there is always a desire to express it." —*3 Testimonies, pp. 543:1–544:0.*

"Day by day we are to fight the good fight of faith. Day by day God will give us our work; and though we cannot see the end from the beginning, we are to examine ourselves daily to see if we are in the path of righteousness. We must strive to overcome, looking unto Jesus; for in every temptation He will be at our side to give us victory. Every day should come to us as the last day in which we may be privileged to work for God, and much of it must be given to prayer that we may work in the strength of Christ. This is the way in which Enoch walked with God, warning and condemning the world by manifesting before them a righteous character."—*Review and Herald, August 18, 1891, para. 6.*

"By the blessings and honors which He bestowed upon Enoch, the Lord teaches a lesson of the greatest importance, that all will be rewarded, who by faith rely upon the promised Sacrifice, and faithfully obey God's commandments. Here, again, two classes are represented which were to exist until the Second Coming of Christ—the righteous and the wicked, the loyal and the rebellious. God will remember the righteous, who fear Him. On account of His dear Son, he will respect and honor them, and give them everlasting life. But the wicked, who trample upon his authority, He will destroy from the earth, and they will be as though they had not been."—*Signs of the Times, February 20, 1879, para. 8.*

"Never are we to rely upon worldly recognition and rank. Never are we, in the establishment of institutions, to try to compete with worldly institutions in size or splendor. The great desire of the managers of our sanitariums should be to walk in obedience to the Lord that all the helpers connected with these institutions can by faith walk with God as did Enoch."—*Medical Ministry, p. 158:2.*

"God ever commends obedience. For his obedience Enoch was translated to heaven, and Noah was saved from the flood that deluged the earth. 'Behold,' writes the psalmist, 'the eye of the Lord is upon them that fear Him, upon them that hope in His mercy; to deliver their soul from death, and to keep them alive in famine.' 'I have seen the wicked in great power, and spreading himself like a green bay tree. Yet he passed away, and lo, he was not; yea, I sought him, but he could not be found. Mark the perfect man, and behold the upright; for the end of that man is peace. But the transgressors shall be destroyed together; the end of the wicked shall be cut off.' "—*Signs of the Times, February 11, 1897, para. 15.*

"Men who, like Enoch, are walking in the light of Christ, will exercise self-control, even under temptation and provocation. Although tried by the perversity and obstinacy of others, they dare not let impulse bear sway. If you are walking in the light, you will give evidence of divine power combined with human effort, and others will see that you are led and taught by God. You will feel that the Holy Watcher is by your side taking knowledge of your words."—*Medical Ministry, p. 206:2.*

"What is God's law?—It is the expression of His character. What is service?—The work that human beings are to do for Christ. By wearing the yoke of obedience, we may be laborers together with Him. Through perfect obedience Enoch walked with God. The life in which the mind, soul, heart, and strength are given to God forms a part of the divine plan."—*Signs of the Times, June 16, 1898, para. 8.*

"The Lord's claims extend to our words and actions. Even thoughts must be brought into captivity to Christ. Then the whole life is a witness for the right. God's true servants subordinate every act to the universal law of obedience. 'Lord, what wilt Thou have me to do?' is the inquiry of the soul. They keep their eyes directed heavenward, that they may be approved of God, workmen that need not to be ashamed. They maintain a watching, praying attitude. They remember the words, 'Ye are not your own; for ye are bought with a price: therefore glorify God in your body, and in your spirit, which are God's.' Thus Enoch walked with God, constantly realizing his accountability."—*Youth's Instructor, August 17, 1899, para. 8.*

Chapter 9
The Purity of Enoch

"Enoch's life and character, which were so holy that he was translated to heaven without seeing death, represent what the lives and characters of all must be, if, like Enoch, they are to be translated when Christ shall come. His life was what the life of every individual may be if he closely connects with God. We should remember that Enoch was surrounded with influences so depraved that God brought the flood of waters on the world to destroy its inhabitants for their corruption."—*Our High Calling, p. 278:2.*

"Some few in every generation from Adam resisted his [Satan's] artifice and stood forth as noble representatives of what it was in the power of man to do and to be—Christ working with human efforts, helping man in overcoming the power of Satan. Enoch and Elijah are the correct representatives of what the race might become through faith in Jesus Christ if they chose to be. Satan was greatly disturbed because these noble, holy men stood untainted amid the moral pollution surrounding them, perfected righteous characters, and were accounted worthy for translation to heaven. As they stood forth in moral power in noble uprightness, overcoming Satan's temptations, he could not bring them under the dominion of death. He triumphed that he had power to overcome Moses with his temptations, and that he could mar his illustrious character and lead him to the sin of taking glory to himself before the people which belonged to God."—*3 Selected Messages, pp. 146:5–147:0.*

"Enoch's righteous life was in marked contrast with the wicked people around him. His piety, his purity, his unswerving integrity were the result of his walking with God, while the wickedness of the world was the result of their walking with the deceiver of mankind. There never has been and never will be an age when the moral darkness will be so dense as when Enoch lived a

41

life of irreproachable righteousness."—*Sons and Daughters of God, p. 20:3.*

"We are living amid the perils of the last days, and we must receive our strength from the same source as did Enoch. We must walk with God. A separation from the world is required of us. We cannot remain free from this pollution unless we follow the example of faithful Enoch and walk with God. But how many are slaves to the lust of the flesh, and the lust of the eye, and the pride of life?"—*Sermons and Talks, Volume Two, p. 5:6.*

"Were Enoch upon the earth today, his heart would be in harmony with all of God's requirements; he would walk with God, although surrounded by influences the most wicked and debasing. The palm tree well represents the life of a Christian. It stands upright amid the burning desert sands, and dies not; for it draws sustenance from springs beneath the surface."—*Reflecting Christ, p. 307:4.*

"Many have not had that religious experience that is essential for them, that they may stand without fault before the throne of God. The furnace fires of affliction He permits to be kindled upon them to consume the dross, to refine, to purify and cleanse from the defilement of sin, of self love, and to bring them to know God and to become acquainted with Jesus by walking with Him as did Enoch."—*In Heavenly Places, p. 87:2.*

"There is to be a people fitted up for translation to heaven, whom Enoch represents. They are looking and waiting for the coming of the Lord. The work will go on with those who will cooperate with Jesus in the work of redemption. He gave Himself for us that He might redeem us from all iniquity and purify unto Himself a peculiar people, zealous of good works. God has made every provision that they should be intelligent Christians, filled with a knowledge of His will in all wisdom and spiritual understanding."—*Testimony on Sexual Behavior, Adultery, and Divorce, p. 86:3.*

"If you come into close relationship to Jesus Christ you see wondrous things out of His law that are not now seen. The softening, subduing influence of the Spirit of God upon human hearts and minds will make the true children of God to sit together in heavenly places in Christ Jesus. Christian culture will be carried on in every heart by the Holy Spirit. There will be a soft, subdued spirit in all those who are looking unto Jesus. The love of Jesus always leads to Christian courtesy, refinement of language, and purity of expression that testify the company we are with—that like Enoch we are walking with God. There is no storming, no harshness, but a sweet fragrance in speech and in spirit."—*That I May Know Him, p. 198:2.*

" 'And Enoch walked with God.' This is the path of safety to all who profess to follow Christ, but in a special manner to those who profess to be watchmen upon the walls of Zion. I am deeply convinced that there must be greater piety among those who teach the truth of God. Those who labor for the truth in word and doctrine should closely examine themselves for the purpose of purifying and improving their character. Many study books to perfect themselves in knowledge, while they neglect to become acquainted with themselves. Christ said, in the prayer just prior to His betrayal, 'I sanctify myself, that they also might be sanctified through the truth.' If the minister would present those for whom he labors, perfect in Christ, he must himself be perfect. This work of becoming perfect through the merits of Christ requires much meditation and earnest prayer."—*Review and Herald, August 8, 1878, para 1.*

Chapter 10
The Growth of Enoch

"Man is not what he might be and what it is God's will that he should be. The strong power of Satan upon the human race keeps them upon a low level; but this need not be so, else Enoch could not have become so elevated and ennobled as to walk with God. Man need not cease to grow intellectually and spiritually during his lifetime. But the minds of many are so occupied with themselves and their own selfish interests as to leave no room for higher and nobler thoughts. And the standard of intellectual as well as spiritual attainments is far too low. With many, the more responsible the position they occupy, the better pleased are they with themselves; and they cherish the idea that the position gives character to the man. Few realize that they have a constant work before them to develop forbearance, sympathy, charity, consciousness, and fidelity,—traits of character indispensable to those who occupy positions of responsibility."—*4 Testimonies, pp. 547:3–548:0.*

"Christ came into the world to save it, to connect fallen man with the infinite God. Christ's followers are to be channels of light. Maintaining communion with God, they are to transmit to those in darkness and error the choice blessings which they receive of heaven. Enoch did not become polluted with the iniquities existing in his day; why need we in our day? But we may, like our Master, have compassion for suffering humanity, pity for the unfortunate, and generous consideration for the feelings and necessities of the needy, the troubled, and the despairing." —*5 Testimonies, p. 113:2.*

"If the Christian minister receives the golden oil, he has life; and where there is life, there is no stagnation, no dwarfed experience. There is constant growth to the full stature of Christ Jesus. If we have a deep, growing experience in heavenly things, we walk with the Lord, as did Enoch. Instead of consenting to the propositions of Satan, there is most earnest prayer for the heavenly anointing, that we may distinguish the right, the heaven born, from the common."—*Testimonies to Ministers, pp. 338:2–339:0.*

"Be men of God, on the gaining side. Knowledge is within the reach of all who desire it. God designs the mind shall become strong, thinking deeper, fuller, clearer. Walk with God as did Enoch; make God your counselor and you cannot but make improvement."—*Mind, Character, and Personality, Volume 1, p. 226:6.*

Chapter 11
The Humility of Enoch

"Those who have experienced the cleansing efficacy of the blood of Christ upon their hearts will be like their Master, pure, peaceable, and lowly of heart. No matter how bold and earnest one may be in his claims of spiritual soundness, and perfection of character, if he lacks Christian grace and humility, the dregs of the disease of sin is in his nature, and unless it is purged from him, he cannot enter the kingdom of heaven. The truly holy, who walk with God like Enoch of old, will not be boastful of their purity, but be courteous, humble, unselfish, free from spiritual pride and exaltation. Those who know most of God, and keep their eye fixed on the Author and Finisher of their faith will see nothing good or great in themselves. They will feel, after doing all in their power to be faithful, that they are yet unprofitable servants."—*Life Sketches of James and Ellen White, (1888 edition), p. 211:3.*

"It is true greatness, it is nobility of soul and meekness and lowliness of heart, which will bring us into such a position before God that we can receive the finishing touch of immortality, and be translated as was Enoch."—*Review and Herald, December 12, 1878, para. 2.*

"Christ says: 'Come unto Me, all ye that labor and are heavy laden, and I will give you rest. Take My yoke upon you, and learn of Me; for I am meek and lowly in heart; and ye shall find rest unto your souls. For My yoke is easy, and My burden is light.' He who cherishes pride and selfish feelings will show that he is seeking self-exaltation in the little and larger things of life. Those who are really worthy of attention and preference will never be found putting themselves forward, but will leave the best and highest places for someone else, esteeming others better than themselves. Yet the very modesty and humility of character cannot be hid. The person who is willing to be little and unknown will be esteemed, for his life will be fragrant with unselfish actions. He will not be ostentatious, and seek to impress upon others in a lower position that he is vastly their superior. Grace works quietly and steadily, and educates the believing soul in such a way that he conforms to principles upon which a well-directed education is founded. It is the Spirit of God that works to mold and fashion the human agent through acts oft repeated, to the model of Christ's character. Faithful in little things, the Christian pays strict attention to the smallest matters, and thus forms a character that will lead him to be faithful in great matters. He possesses the faith that works by love and purifies the soul. God has made us His own by creation and redemption, and if we are willing to occupy a lowly position in this life, are content to be little and unknown, we shall have full recognition in the future life. Our Redeemer will say, 'Child, come up higher.' God has caused the sun to bless with its light not only the mountain heights, but the lowly valleys and plains, and He will cause the beams of the Sun of Righteousness to fill the souls of those who are humble and contrite, whose spirit is meek and lowly. The love and grace of Christ will fill the soul of him who humbly walks with God as did Enoch. It is in proportion as the heart is sanctified by grace, and filled with active love for God and for our fellowmen, that we do nothing for show or by compulsion. Those who love God do that which is pleasant for them to do, and that is to reveal God in character, and submit the whole heart to the sanctification of the truth."—*Review and Herald, October 8, 1895, para. 6.*

"Keep your soul in the love of God, and make straight paths for your feet, lest the lame be turned out of the way. Keep your taper kindled from the divine altar, and then let your light shine to others. Let your confidence be wholly in the Lord. Learn meekness and lowliness of heart. You need to put your entire trust in Jesus Christ. He is the only safe Teacher. The great question now is the salvation of the soul. If you walk with Christ, you learn wisdom by communion with Him, as did Enoch."—*Manuscript Releases, Volume Eight, p. 10:1.*

Chapter 12
The Love of Enoch

"Enoch, we read, walked with God three hundred years. That was a long time to be in communion with Him…. He communed with God because it was agreeable to him,…and he loved the society of God."—*Conflict and Courage, p. 29:2.*

"Enoch walked with God three hundred years before his translation to Heaven. He had the daily testimony that his ways pleased God. Why should not every Christian follow Christ as did this faithful servant? Do you love Jesus a great way off? Do the tidings of His coming seem a message of joy to your heart? Do you find His service a profitable service? How can you win others to truth, if your own heart is not in the work, and you do not see matchless charms in your Redeemer? The prayer of Christ was that He might be glorified in those He had left on earth to carry on His work, and we do not glorify our Redeemer when we complain of the difficulties of the way, and murmur at the providences of God." —*Signs of the Times, February 3, 1888, para. 13.*

Chapter 13
The Walk of Enoch

"Christ commands His followers to walk in the light. Walking means moving onward, exerting ourselves, exercising our ability, being actively engaged. Unless we exercise ourselves in the good work to which our Saviour has called us, and feel the importance of personal effort in this work, we shall have a sickly, stunted religion. We gain new victories by our own experience in working. We gain activity and strength by walking in the light, that we may have energy to run in the way of God's commandments. We may gain an increase of strength at every step we advance heavenward. God will bless His people only when they try to be a blessing to others. Our graces are matured and developed by exercise."—*3 Testimonies, pp. 436:2–437:0.*

"Enoch, we read, walked with God three hundred years. That was a long time to be in communion with Him…. He communed with God. When we do this, our faces will be lighted up by the brightness of His presence, and when we meet another, we shall speak of His power, saying, Praise God. Good is the Lord, and good is the Word of the Lord."—*Manuscript 17, 1903.*

"Did he [Enoch] see God by his side? Only by faith. He knew that the Lord was there, and he adhered steadfastly to the principles of truth. We, too, are to walk with God." *Manuscript 17, 1903.*

"Enoch walked with God, while of the world around him sacred history records. 'And God saw that the wickedness of man was great in the earth, and that every imagination of the thoughts of his heart was only evil continually.' Enoch's righteous life was in marked contrast with the wicked people around him. His piety, his purity, his unswerving integrity were the result of his walking with God, while the wickedness of the world was the result of their walking with the deceiver of mankind. There never has been and never will be an age when the moral darkness will be so dense

as when Enoch lived a life of irreproachable righteousness."
—*Manuscript 43, 1900.*

" 'We all, with open face beholding as in a glass the glory of the Lord, are changed into the same image from glory to glory, even as by the Spirit of the Lord.' We are to keep the Lord ever before us. Those who do this, walk with God as did Enoch, and imperceptibly to themselves, they become one with the Father and with the Son. Day by day a change is wrought upon mind and hearts, and the natural inclination, the natural ways, are molded after God's ways and Spirit. They increase in spiritual knowledge, and are growing up to the full stature of men and women in Christ Jesus. They reflect to the world the character of Christ, and abiding in Him, and He in them, they fulfill the mission for which they were called to be the children of God,—they become the light of the world, a city set upon a hill that cannot be covered.... Those who have been lightened from above send forth the bright beams of the Sun of Righteousness."—*Youth's Instructor, October 25, 1894, 10.*

"You rely upon your good intentions and resolutions, and the principal sum of life is composed of resolutions made and resolutions broken. What you all need is to die to self, cease clinging to self, and surrender to God.... Look away from yourselves to Jesus. He is all and in all. The merits of the blood of a crucified and risen Saviour will avail to cleanse you from the least and greatest sin. In trusting faith commit the keeping of your souls to God as unto a faithful Creator. Be not in continual fear and apprehension that God will leave you. He never will unless you depart from Him. Christ will come in and dwell with you if you will open the door of your hearts to Him. There may be perfect harmony between you and the Father and His Son if you will die to self and live unto God.

"How few are aware that they have darling idols, that they have cherished sins! God sees these sins to which you may be blinded, and He works with His pruning knife to strike deep and separate these cherished sins from you.... How hard it is for you to submit to the crucifixion of self; but when the work is all submitted to God, to Him who knows our weakness and our sinfulness, He takes the very best way to bring about the desired results. It was through constant conflict and simple faith that Enoch walked with God. You may all do the same. You may be thoroughly converted and transformed, and be indeed children of God, enjoying not only the knowledge of His will, but by your example, leading others in the same path of humble obedience and consecration."—*3 Testimonies, pp. 542:3–543:1.*

"We bear about in our body the dying of the Lord Jesus, which is life and salvation and righteousness to us. Wherever we go, there is the recollection of One dear to us. We are abiding in Christ by a living faith. He is abiding in our hearts by individual appropriating of faith. We have the companionship of the divine presence, and as we realize this presence, our thoughts are brought into captivity to Jesus Christ. Our spiritual exercises are in accordance with the vividness of our sense of this companionship. Enoch walked with God in this way; and Christ is dwelling in our hearts by faith when we will consider what He is to us, and what a work He has wrought out for us in the plan of redemption. We shall be most happy in cultivating a sense of this great gift of God to our world and to us personally.

"These thoughts have a controlling power upon the whole character. I want to impress upon your mind that you may have a divine Companion with you, if you will, always…. As the mind dwells upon Christ, the character is molded after the divine similitude. The thoughts are pervaded with a sense of His goodness, His love. We contemplate His character, and thus He is in all our thoughts. His love encloses us…. We cannot see anything else, or talk of anything else…. By beholding, we are conformed to the divine similitude, even the likeness of Christ. To all with whom we associate we reflect the bright and cheerful beams of His righteousness. We have become transformed in character, for heart, soul, mind, are irradiated by the reflection of Him who loved us and gave Himself for us."—*Testimonies to Ministers, pp. 388:1–389:0.*

"In faith they [Daniel and his friends] prayed for wisdom, and they lived their prayers. They placed themselves where God could bless them. They avoided that which would weaken their powers, and improved every opportunity to become intelligent in all lines of learning. They followed the rules of life that could not fail to give them strength of intellect. They sought to acquire knowledge for one purpose—that they might honor God. They realized that in order to stand as representatives of true religion amid the false religions of heathenism they must have clearness of intellect and must perfect a Christian character. And God Himself was their teacher. Constantly praying, conscientiously studying, keeping in touch with the Unseen, they walk with God as did Enoch.

"True success in any line of work is not the result of chance or accident or destiny. It is the outworking of God's providences, the reward of faith and discretion, of virtue and perseverance. Fine mental qualities and a high moral tone are not the result of accident. God gives opportunities; success depends upon the use made of them."—*Prophets and Kings, p. 486:1–2.*

"Enoch not only meditated and prayed, and put on the armor of watchfulness, but he came forth from his pleadings with God to plead with his fellow men. He did not mask the truth to find favor with unbelievers, thus neglecting their souls. This close connection with God gave him courage to work the works of God. Enoch walked with God, and 'had the testimony that his ways pleased God.' This is the privilege of every believer today. It is man dwelling with God, and God taking up His abode with man. 'I in them, and thou in me,' says Jesus. To walk with God and have the witness that their ways please Him is an experience not to be confined to Enoch, to Elijah, to patriarchs, to prophets, to apostles, and to martyrs. It is not only the privilege but the duty of every follower of Christ to have Jesus enshrined in the heart, to carry Him with them in their lives; and they will indeed be fruit-bearing trees."—*Manuscript 43, August 2, 1900,* "The Prophet Enoch."—*The Upward Look, p. 228:4.*

"How little is said of Enoch; how brief is his biography! Many volumes are written of Napoleon; much is said of Caesar and other great men of the world. Their exploits are recorded and sent through the length and breadth of the land; yet we have no evidence that these men honored God or that God honored them. Of Enoch it is recorded, 'Enoch walked with God: and he was not: for God took him.' "—*Review and Herald, April 15, 1909, para. 3.*

"We may have a knowledge of the truth, but this is not enough. We must bring its living principles into our lives, and it must sanctify our characters and flow out to others. If we ourselves are conscious that our lives are not right, how can we help those who are around us? How can we have faith to come to God for help? The belief in Jesus is to be of that divine character that will bring Jesus into our life and actions, and will flow out in righteous actions to others. When we do this we will have an influence for good on all around us. The God of heaven understands all about the difficulties that we have to meet in this world, which are no more favorable for the perfection of Christian character than when Enoch was in the world. And yet Enoch walked with God, and communed with God, and God communed with him. He kept God's commandments. He kept in mind that the God of heaven was by his side, and he must do nothing to grieve his Lord. The Lord honored Enoch, and translated him to heaven without seeing death."—*Review and Herald, May 3, 1887, para. 10.*

" 'Blessed are the pure in heart: for they shall see God' (Matt 5:8). How would they see God? In the way that Enoch saw Him. They had the privilege of walking and talking with God. By faith Enoch lived in the presence of God three hundred years. By faith he saw the faith of Jesus. He was taken into special favor with Him. The priests and rulers needed just such an experience as Enoch had. They needed a continual sense of the presence of God. Oh what riches of grace the Lord longed to bestow upon the favored people of God. It is represented in the call to the supper prepared for them. 'All things are ready: come' (Matt 22:4)." —*Manuscript 96, September 23, 1879*, "The Jews' Rejection of Christ."—*This Day with God, p. 275:3.*

"While trusting in your heavenly Father for the help you need, He will not leave you. God has a heaven full of blessings that He wants to bestow on those who are earnestly seeking for that help which the Lord alone can give. It was in looking in faith to Jesus, in asking of Him, in believing that every word spoken would be verified, that Enoch walked with God. He kept close by the side of God, obeying His every word…. His was a wonderful life of oneness. Christ was his Companion. He was in intimate fellowship with God (*MS 111, 1898*)."—*S.D.A. Bible Commentary, Vol. 1, p. 1087/2:3.*

"We are to recognize Christ. He does not want us to be as a band of mourners in a funeral train, bearing upon us the marks of care and perplexity. He wants us to commit the keeping of our souls to Him. He wants us to put our trust in the naked promise. But, you say, I do not feel like it. Tell me what value there is in feeling! Is feeling stronger than the faith which it is your privilege to exercise in God? Feelings change with almost every circumstance; but the promises of the Eternal are as solid rock. Let us build our house upon the sure foundation, and rivet our souls to the eternal Rock, the Rock of Ages. If we do this, we shall find that it will become habitual for us to remember that we have a Companion. Wherever we are, we are to talk with God. This is the way Enoch walked with God. He talked with Him. He recognized the Divine Presence. And in the days of Enoch the world was no more favorable for the perfection of Christian character than in 1901."—*General Conference Bulletin, April 4, 1901, para. 13.*

"He who continually communes with God, as did Enoch, will converse of the majesty of God. Enoch kept His mind continually fixed upon God. He lived in an age which was no more conducive to piety than is our own. The Lord will walk with anyone who chooses His companionship. He invites you to come. He says: 'Come unto Me, all ye that labor and are heavy laden, and I will give you rest. Take My yoke upon you, and learn of Me; for I am meek and lowly in heart, and ye shall find rest unto your souls.' What an exalted privilege is it to bear the yoke with Christ, for He says, 'My yoke is easy, and My burden is light.' "—*Sabbath School Worker, April 1, 1895, para. 2.*

"In the repentant Adam a voice was raised to testify that God is true, that His law is not to be broken, and that his Word cannot be disregarded with impunity. Enoch walked with God three hundred years. He was a man of wisdom, enlightened and taught of God. He was daily proving his divine Companion, who, in turn, was testing Enoch. This witness was brought into singular nearness to God, and was constantly seeking His guidance. He was a man of infinite wisdom, because he relied on infinite wisdom. He was a man of great meekness and humility, because he trusted in

God for all things, and not in himself. He did not walk slowly and reluctantly, but kept pace with the opening providences of God."—*The Youth's Instructor, February 25, 1897, para. 2.*

"As we walk the streets with those who care not for God or heaven or heavenly things, we can talk to them of Jesus. We have something more precious than they to look upon—it is Jesus. He is with us in the moral darkness of this age. We can tell Him of the afflictions of our soul and the wickedness in the world and none of these things need hinder us. We can talk with Jesus. We can talk with Jesus as Enoch talked with God. He could tell his Lord all about his trials. Here was the way Enoch walked with God, and when light shone out upon his pathway, he did not expect to say, 'Why, what will my friends and relatives say of me if I take this course?' No, he did that which was right whatever the consequence."—*Manuscript Releases, Volume Nine, p. 256:3.*

"In acquiring the wisdom of the Babylonians, Daniel and his companions were far more successful than their fellow students; but their learning did not come by chance. They obtained their knowledge by the faithful use of their powers, under the guidance of the Holy Spirit. They placed themselves in connection with the Source of all wisdom, making the knowledge of God the foundation of their education. In faith they prayed for wisdom, and they lived their prayers. They placed themselves where God could bless them. They avoided that which would weaken their powers, and improved every opportunity to become intelligent in all lines of learning. They followed the rules of life that could not fail to give them strength of intellect. They sought to acquire knowledge for one purpose—that they might honor God. They realized that in order to stand as representatives of true religion amid the false religions of heathenism they must have clearness of intellect and must perfect a Christian character. And God Himself was their teacher. Constantly praying, conscientiously studying, keeping in touch with the Unseen, they walked with God as did Enoch." —*Prophets and Kings, p. 486:1.*

"Our present work is to come out from the world and be separate. This is the only way we can walk with God, as did Enoch."—*Conflict and Courage, p. 29:7.*

"I wish I could impress upon every worker the great need of continual, earnest prayer. They cannot be constantly upon their knees, but they can be uplifting their hearts to God. This is the way that Enoch walked with God. When young, or even married men and women open their family secrets to you, beware. When they express a desire for sympathy, know that it is time to exercise great caution. Those who are imbued with the Spirit of God, will have no unholy repining for sympathy. They have a companionship that satisfies every desire of mind and heart."—*Signs of the Times, October 15, 1885, para. 5.*

"It is our privilege to walk as did Enoch. Christ has assured us that those who walk in His steps are His disciples, His true representatives. He says, 'I am the Light of the world; he that followeth Me shall not walk in darkness, but shall have the Light of life.' Is not this sufficient assurance? Should not these words fill us with holy peace and joy?"—*Signs of the Times, October 4, 1899, para. 2.*

"They [Daniel and his companions] were very careful to keep themselves in touch with God. They prayed and studied, and brought into their practical life strictly conscientious, humble minds. They walked with God as did Enoch. The Word of the Lord was their meat and their drink. 'And in all matters of wisdom and understanding, that the king inquired of them, he found them ten times better than all the magicians and astrologers that were in all his realm.' "—*Medical Ministry, p. 276:3.*

"Before we can enter the heavenly courts, we must be refined, purified, elevated, and ennobled. In order to preserve the purity which God requires, the truth must be brought into constant contact with mind and heart. God calls upon His people to walk with Him, as did Enoch. Study His Word, if you desire to have Christ abiding in you, the life blood of the soul."—*The Signs of the Times, September 18, 1901, para. 12.*

Chapter 14
The Separation of Enoch

"This lesson is for us to study carefully. We are in no case to swerve from our allegiance. No duties that God presents before us should cause us to work at cross-purposes with Him. The Word of God is to be our counselor. It is only those who render perfect and thorough obedience to God that He will choose. Those who follow the Lord are to be firm and straightforward in obeying His directions. Any deviations to follow human devising or planning disqualifies them for being trustworthy. Even if they have to walk as did Enoch,—with God alone,—His children must separate from those who do not obey Him, who show that they are not in vital connection with Him. The Lord God is a Host; and all who are in His service will realize the meaning of His words to Zerubbabel, 'Not by my might, nor by power, but by My Spirit, saith the Lord of hosts' (*Youth's Instructor, April 28, 1898*)." —*S.D.A. Bible Commentary, Vol. 2, p. 1037/1:4–2:0.*

"If the Christian thrives and progresses at all, he must do so amid strangers to God, amid scoffing, subject to ridicule. He must stand upright like the palm tree in the desert. The sky may be as brass, the desert sand may beat about the palm tree's roots, and pile itself in heaps about its trunk. Yet the tree lives as an evergreen, fresh and vigorous amid the burning sands. Remove the sand till you reach the rootlets of the palm tree, and you discover the secret of its life; it strikes down deep beneath the surface, to the secret waters hidden in the earth. Christians indeed may be fitly represented by the palm tree. They are like Enoch; although surrounded by corrupting influences, their faith takes hold of the Unseen. They walk with God, deriving strength and grace from Him to withstand the moral pollution surrounding them. Like Daniel in the courts of Babylon, they stand pure and uncontaminated; their life is hid with Christ in God. They are virtuous in spirit amid depravity; they are true and loyal, fervent and zealous, while surrounded by infidels, hypocritical professors, godless and worldly men. Their faith and life are hid with Christ in God. Jesus is in them a well of water springing up into everlasting life. Faith, like the rootlets of the palm tree, penetrates beneath the things which are seen, drawing spiritual nourishment from the Fountain of life (*Signs of the Times, July 8, 1886*)." —*S.D.A. Bible Commentary, Vol. 3, p. 1151/1:4–2:0.*

"Enoch, separating himself from the world, and spending much of his time in prayer and in communion with God, represents God's loyal people in the last days who will be separate from the world. Unrighteousness will prevail to a dreadful extent upon the earth. Men will give themselves up to every imagination of their corrupt hearts, and carry out their deceptive philosophy, and rebel against the authority of high Heaven."—*Spirit of Prophecy, Vol. 1, p. 64:3.*

Chapter 15
The Sociality of Enoch

"Enoch was a marked character, and many look upon his life as something above what the generality of mortals can ever reach. But Enoch's life and character...represent the lives and characters of all who will be translated when Christ shall come. His life was what the life of every individual may be if he will live near to God. We should remember that Enoch was surrounded by unholy influences."—*Signs of the Times, November 11, 1886, para. 5.*

"Enoch was a holy man. He served God with singleness of heart. He realized the corruptions of the human family and separated himself from the descendants of Cain and reproved them for their great wickedness. There were those upon the earth who acknowledged God, who feared and worshiped Him. Yet righteous Enoch was so distressed with the increasing wickedness of the ungodly, that he would not daily associate with them, fearing that he should be affected by their infidelity and that his thoughts might not ever regard God with that holy reverence which was due His exalted character. His soul was vexed as he daily witnessed their trampling upon the authority of God. He chose to be separate from them, and spent much of his time in solitude, which he devoted to reflection and prayer."—*Story of Redemption, pp. 57:2–58:0.*

"The character of the one who thus beholds Christ is so like His, that one looking at him sees Christ's own character shining out as from a mirror. Imperceptibly to ourselves we are changed day by day from our own ways and will into the ways and will of Christ, into the loveliness of His character. Thus we grow up into Christ, and unconsciously reflect His image."—*Our High Calling, p. 58:3.*

"Enoch kept the Lord ever before him, and the Inspired Word says that he 'walked with God.' He made Christ his constant companion. He was in the world, and performed his duties to the world; but he was ever under the influence of Jesus. He reflected Christ's character, exhibiting the same qualities of goodness, mercy, tender compassion, sympathy, forbearance, meekness, humility, and love. His association with Christ day by day transformed him into the image of Him whom he was so intimately connected. Day by day he was growing away from his own way into Christ's way, the heavenly, the divine, in his thoughts and feelings. He was constantly inquiring, Is this the way of the Lord? His was a constant growth, and he had fellowship with the Father and the Son. This is genuine sanctification."—*6 Bible commentary, pp. 1097/2:4–1098/1:0.*

"God did not intend that His people, in self-righteous exclusiveness, should shut themselves away from the world, so that they could have no influence upon it. Like their Master, the followers of Christ in every age were to be the light of the world…'Let your light so shine before men, that they may see your good works, and glorify your Father which is in heaven.' Matthew 5:16. This is just what Enoch, and Noah, Abraham, Joseph, and Moses did. It is just what God designed that His people Israel should do."—*Patriarchs and Prophets, pp. 369:3–370:0.*

"Those who will put on the whole armor of God and devote some time every day to meditation and prayer and to the study of the Scriptures will be connected with heaven, and will have a saving, transforming influence upon those around them. Great thoughts, noble aspirations, clear perceptions of truth and duty to God, will be theirs. They will be yearning for purity, for light, for love, for all the graces of heavenly birth. Their earnest prayers will enter into that within the veil. This class will have a sanctified boldness to come into the presence of the infinite One. They will feel that heaven's light and glories are for them, and they will become refined, elevated, ennobled by this intimate acquaintance with God. Such is the privilege of true Christians.

"Abstract meditation is not enough; busy action is not enough; both are essential to the formation of Christian character. Strength acquired in earnest, secret prayer prepares us to withstand the allurements of society ..

"Christ's followers are to be channels of light. Maintaining communion with God, they are to transmit to those in darkness and error the choice blessings which they receive of heaven. Enoch did not become polluted with the iniquities existing in his day; why need we in our day? But we may, like our Master, have compassion for suffering humanity, pity for the unfortunate, and a generous consideration for the feelings and necessities of the needy, the troubled, and the despairing.

"Those who are Christians indeed will seek to do good to others and at the same time will so order their conversation and deportment as to maintain a calm, hallowed peace of mind. God's Word requires that we should be like our Saviour, that we should bear His image, imitate His example, live His life."—*5 Testimonies, pp. 112:4–113:3.*

"Let the soul in living faith fasten upon God. Let the tongue speak His praise. When you associate together, let the mind be reverently turned to contemplation of eternal realities. Thus you will be helping one another to be spiritually minded. When your will is in harmony with the divine will, you will be in harmony with one another; you will have Christ by your side as a counselor.

"Enoch walked with God. So may every laborer for Christ. You may say with the psalmist, 'I have set the Lord always before me. Because He is at my right hand I shall not be moved.' (Psalm 16:8). While you feel that you have no sufficiency of yourself, your sufficiency will be in Jesus. If you expect all your counsel and wisdom to come from men, mortal and finite like yourself, you will receive only human help. If you go to God for help and wisdom, He will never disappoint your faith."—*Gospel Workers, pp. 417:4–418:0.*

" 'By faith Enoch was translated that he should not see death, and was not found, because God had translated him, for before his translation he had this testimony, that he pleased God." —*Hebrews 11:5.*

"The work of God is sacred and calls for men of lofty integrity. Men are wanted whose sense of justice, even in the smallest matters, will not allow them to make an entry of their time that is not minute and correct,—men who will realize that they are handling means that belongs to God, and who would not unjustly appropriate one cent to their own use; men who will be just as faithful and exact, careful and diligent, in their labor, in the absence of their employer as in his presence, proving by their faithfulness that they are not merely men-pleasers, eye-servants, but are conscientious, faithful, true workmen, doing right, not for human praise, but because they love and choose the right from a high sense of their obligation to God."—*3 Testimonies, p. 25:1.*

"Surrounded with influences so corrupt that God brought a flood of water upon the earth to destroy its inhabitants for their wickedness, Enoch was by no means free from temptation; yet in the midst of a society no more friendly to righteousness than that which surrounds us, he lived a life of holiness. Breathing an atmosphere tainted with sin and corruption, he remained unsullied by the prevailing iniquity of the age. For three hundred years he 'walked with God.' "—*Signs of the Times, October 12, 1904, para. 2.*

"Enoch did not close himself within monastic walls in order to keep pure. He did not build up a wall of separation between himself and his fellow men. Had he done so, the world would not have seen his light, that God was manifest in him. He was to reveal what man may be when connected with the Source of all power. He had home religion. He walked with God when engaged in his business, and in the associations of his daily life. He was a husband and father, and he exemplified what a husband and father should be under the guidance and control of Christ."—*The Youth's Instructor, February, 25, 1897, para. 3.*

"Adam, Enoch, and Noah were representative men. Jesus himself was their educator. God did not design that they should build a wall of seclusion around themselves. They were to be light-bearers, representing Christ, and thus representatives of God. These men in their day were to do just as Christ enjoined upon His disciples when He was among them as their teacher. His words to them were: 'Ye are the light of the world. A city that is set on a hill cannot be hid…. Let your light so shine before men, that they may see your good words, and glorify your Father which is in heaven.' "—*Youth's Instructor, February 25, 1897, para. 6.*

Chapter 16
The Warnings of Enoch

"Enoch became a preacher of righteousness, making known to the people what God had revealed to him. Those who feared the Lord sought out this holy man, to share his instruction and his prayers. He labored publicly also, bearing God's messages to all who would hear the words of warning. His labors were not restricted to the Sethites. In the land where Cain had sought to flee from the Divine Presence, the prophet of God made known the wonderful scenes that had passed before his vision. 'Behold,' he declared, 'the Lord cometh with ten thousands of His saints, to execute judgment upon all, and to convince all that are ungodly among them of all their ungodly deeds.' Jude 14–15.

"He was a fearless reprover of sin. While he preached the love of God in Christ to the people of his time, and pleaded with them to forsake their evil ways, he rebuked the prevailing iniquity and warned the men of his generation that judgment would surely be visited upon the transgressor. It was the Spirit of Christ that spoke through Enoch; that Spirit is manifested, not alone in utterances of love, compassion, and entreaty; it is not smooth things only that are spoken by holy men. God puts into the heart and lips of His messengers truths to utter that are keen and cutting as a two-edged sword."—*Patriarchs and Prophets, 86:1–2.*

"The wickedness of men had reached such a height that destruction was pronounced against them. As year after year passed on, deeper and deeper grew the tide of human guilt, darker and darker gathered the clouds of divine judgment. Yet Enoch, the witness of faith, held on his way, warning, pleading, entreating, striving to turn back the tide of guilt and to stay the bolts of vengeance. Though his warnings were disregarded by a sinful, pleasure-loving people, he had the testimony that God approved, and he continued to battle faithfully against the prevailing evil, until God removed him from a world of sin to the pure joys of heaven."—*Patriarchs and Prophets, 87:1.*

"Those who keep the law of God, like Enoch and Noah, give to the world a message of warning. In Jude we read: 'Enoch also, the seventh from Adam, prophesied of these, saying, Behold, the Lord cometh with ten thousands of His saints, to execute judgment upon all, and to convince all that are ungodly among them of all their ungodly deeds which they have ungodly committed, and of all their hard speeches which ungodly sinners have spoken against him' (verses 14–15)."—*Manuscript Releases, Vol. 18, p. 93:3.*

"Before the destruction of the antediluvian world, Enoch bore his testimony unflinchingly (*Review and Herald, November 1, 1906*)."—*S.D.A. Bible Commentary, Vol. 1, p. 1088/2:2.*

"Enoch in his day sounded the proclamation of the coming of Christ and the execution of judgment upon the unrighteous; and we now see the fulfillment of Enoch's prophecy concerning the great wickedness that should abound. But these who have the light are the very ones commissioned of God to make constantly aggressive warfare. As the inquiry shall be made, 'Watchman, what of the night?' the faithful message is to be heard in response, 'The morning cometh, and also the night.' "—*Testimonies to Ministers, pp. 230:3–231:0.*

"Enoch was an active worker. He did not seek ease and comfort. Nor did he spend his time in idle meditation, or in striving to gain happiness for himself. He did not participate in the festivities and amusements that constantly engaged the attention of the pleasure-lovers of the antediluvian world. In his day the minds of many were absorbed in worldly pleasures,—pleasures that tempted them to go astray. But Enoch was terribly in earnest. With the sinful and with the workers of iniquity he mingled only as God's messenger, to warn them to turn with abhorrence from their evil ways, and to repent and seek God."—*Review and Herald, April 15, 1909, para. 5.*

"As year after year passed, deeper and deeper grew the tide of human guilt, darker and darker gathered the clouds of divine judgment. Yet Enoch, the witness of faith, held on his way, warning, pleading, and teaching, striving to turn back the tide of guilt and to stay the bolts of vengeance."—*8 Testimonies, p. 330:4.*

"God determined to purify the world by a flood; but in mercy and love He gave the antediluvians a probation of one hundred and twenty years. During this time, while the ark was in building, the voices of Noah, Enoch, and many others were heard in warning and entreaty. And every blow struck on the ark was a warning message."—*Australasian Union Conference Record, September 15, 1902, para. 8.*

"It was a hard sentence for Christ to pronounce. It was hard for Him to give up the son of His care. Who can sympathize with Christ in His distress and anguish over the loss of a nation? This was only a symbol of the giving up of a world. Who are so moved by the terrible loss of souls that they have a faint appreciation of the anguish of Christ's soul? Enoch, Noah, Abraham, Moses, David, Jeremiah, and Paul were partakers with Christ in His depths of compassion as far as their human perception could take in the situation. Who can say with Jeremiah, 'Rivers of waters run down mine eyes, because they keep not Thy law? O that my head were waters, and my eyes a fountain of tears, that I might weep day and night for the slain of the daughters of My people.' 'I could wish myself accursed from Christ for my brethren,' Paul exclaimed."—*Bible Training School, September 1, 1908, para. 6.*

"We are the Lord's family, His children, and by Him we are to be instructed in regard to what is and what will be in the future. Vigilant waiting and earnest looking are required in the preparation for the solemn events soon to take place. The perfect man in Christ does not spend all his time in waiting, in meditation and contemplation. While we should have quiet, prayerful hours of meditation when we leave busy bustle and excitement to commune with God, to learn from Him His will concerning us, we are not to forget that we have a positive message of warning to bear to the world. Enoch walked with God. And he bore a message of warning to the inhabitants of the old world. His words and actions, his example of piety, were a continual witness in favor of the truth. In an age no more favorable to the development of a pure, holy character than is the present age, he lived a life of obedience. So filled had the earth become with impurity that the Lord washed it by a flood. He turned the world upside down, as it were, to empty it of its corruption."—*Manuscript Releases, Vol. Twelve, pp. 213:2–214:0.*

Chapter 17
The Message of Enoch

"Enoch was a man of strong and highly cultivated mind and extensive knowledge; he was honored with special revelations from God; yet being in constant communion with Heaven, with a sense of the divine greatness and perfection ever before him, he was one of the humblest of men. The closer the connection with God, the deeper was the sense of his own weakness and imperfection."—*Patriarchs and Prophets, 85:3.*

"Enoch was the first prophet among mankind. He foretold by prophecy the second coming of Christ to our world, and his work at that time. His life was a specimen of Christian consistency. Holy lips alone should speak forth the words of God in denunciation and judgments. His prophecy is not found in the writings of the Old Testament. We may never find any books which relate to the works of Enoch, but Jude, a prophet of God, mentions the work of Enoch."—*Manuscript 43, 1900.*

"Through holy angels God revealed to Enoch His purpose to destroy the world by a flood, and He also opened more fully to him the plan of redemption. By the spirit of prophecy He carried him down through the generations that should live after the Flood, and showed him the great events connected with the second coming of Christ and the end of the world."—*Patriarchs and Prophets, 85:5.*

"Enoch faithfully rehearsed to the people all that God had revealed to him by the Spirit of Prophecy. Some believed his words and turned from their wickedness to fear and worship God."—*Story of Redemption, 59:1.*

"Enoch had been troubled in regard to the dead. It had seemed to him that the righteous and the wicked would go to the dust together, and that this would be their end. He could not see the life of the just beyond the grave. In prophetic vision he was instructed concerning the death of Christ, and was shown His coming in glory, attended by all the holy angels, to ransom His people from the grave. He also saw the corrupt state of the world when Christ should appear the second time—that there would be a boastful, presumptuous, self-willed generation, denying the only God and the Lord Jesus Christ, trampling upon the Law, and despising the atonement. He saw the righteous crowned with glory and honor, and the wicked banished from the presence of the Lord, and destroyed by fire."—*Patriarchs and Prophets, pp. 85:6–86:0.*

"Many died in the faith, not having received the promises [Hebrews 11:39–40]. But having seen them afar off, they believed and confessed that they were strangers and pilgrims on the earth. From the days of Enoch the promises repeated through patriarchs and prophets had kept alive the hope of His appearing."—*Prophets and Kings, p. 700:0.*

"The Saviour's coming was foretold in Eden. When Adam and Eve first heard the promise, they looked for its speedy fulfillment. They joyfully welcomed their first-born son, hoping that he might be the Deliverer. But the fulfillment of the promise tarried. Those who first received it died without the sight. From the days of Enoch the promise was repeated through patriarchs and prophets, keeping alive the hope of his appearing."—*Desire of Ages, p. 31:2.*

"One of the most solemn and yet most glorious truths revealed in the Bible is that of Christ's second coming to complete the great work of redemption. To God's pilgrim people, so long left to sojourn in 'the region and shadow of death,' a precious, joy-inspiring hope is given in the promise of His appearing, who is 'the Resurrection and the Life,' to 'bring home again His banished'…. Holy men of old looked forward to the advent of the Messiah in glory, as the consummation of their hope. Enoch, only the seventh in descent from them that dwelt in Eden, he who for three centuries on earth walked with his God, was permitted to behold from afar the coming of the Deliverer. 'Behold,' he declared, 'the Lord cometh with ten thousands of His saints, to execute judgment upon all.' Jude 14–15."—*Great Controversy, p. 299:1.*

"Enoch was a representative of Christ as surely as was the beloved disciple John. Enoch walked with God, and he was committed the message of the second coming of Christ. 'And Enoch also, the seventh from Adam, prophesied of these saying, Behold, the Lord cometh with ten thousands of His saints, to execute judgment upon all.' Jude 14–15. The message preached by Enoch and his translation to heaven were a convincing argument to all who lived in his time. These things were an argument that Methuselah and Noah could use with power to show that the righteous could be translated.

"The God who walked with Enoch was our Lord and Saviour Jesus Christ. He was the Light of the world then just as He is now. Those who lived then were not without teachers to instruct them in the path of life; for Noah and Enoch were Christians." —*6 Testimonies, p. 392:1–2.*

"Christ was as much man's Redeemer in the beginning of the world as He is today. Before He clothed His divinity with humanity and came to our world, the gospel message was given by Adam, Seth, Enoch, Methuselah, and Noah. Abraham in Canaan and Lot in Sodom bore the message, and from generation to generation faithful messengers proclaimed the Coming One."—*Christ's Object Lessons, p. 126:2.*

"This hope of redemption through the advent of the Son of God as Saviour and King, has never been extinct in the hearts of men. From the beginning there have been some whose faith has reached out beyond the shadows of the present to the realities of the future. Adam, Seth, Enoch, Methuselah, Noah, Shem, Abraham, Isaac, and Jacob—through these and other worthies the Lord has preserved the precious revealings of His will. And it was thus that to the children of Israel, the chosen people through whom was to be imparted a knowledge of the requirements of His Law, and of the salvation to be accomplished through the atoning sacrifice of His beloved Son."—*Prophets and Kings, pp. 682:2–683:0.*

"In every period of this earth's history, God has had His men of opportunity, to whom He has said, 'Ye are My witnesses.' In every age there have been devout men, who gathered up the rays of light as they flashed upon their pathway, and who spoke to the people the words of God. Enoch, Noah, Moses, Daniel, and the long roll of patriarchs and prophets,—these were ministers of righteousness. They were not infallible [in their lives]; they were weak, erring men; but the Lord wrought through them as they gave themselves to His service...

"The stars of heaven are under God's control. He fills them with light. He guides and directs their movements. If He did not, they would become fallen stars. So with His ministers [and all of us]. They are but instruments in His hands, and all the good they accomplish is done through His power."—*Gospel Workers, p. 13:1, 14:0.*

"When men have had every advantage to obtain a knowledge of the truth, how shall plans be laid to keep our laborers from the work of saving souls in the darkness of error? The time is short. Let the message of warning be given clear and distinct. The Lord is coming to execute judgment upon all who obey not the gospel.

"Enoch in his day sounded the proclamation of the coming of Christ and the execution of judgment upon the unrighteous; and we now see the fulfillment of Enoch's prophecy concerning the great wickedness that should abound. But those who have the light are the very ones commissioned of God to make constantly aggressive warfare."—*Testimonies to Ministers, p. 230:2–3.*

"It is our privilege, our duty, to receive light from heaven, that we may perceive the wiles of Satan, and obtain strength to resist his power. Provision has been made for us to come into close connection with Christ and to enjoy the constant protection of the angels of God. Our faith must reach within the veil, where Jesus has entered for us. We must lay hold with firmer grasp on the unfailing promises of God. We must have faith that will not be denied, faith that will take hold of the unseen, faith that is steadfast, immovable. Such faith will bring the blessing of heaven to our souls. The light of the glory of God that shines in the face of Christ may shine upon us, and be reflected upon all around, so that it can be truly said of us, 'Ye are the light of the world.' And it is this connection of the soul with Christ, and this alone, that can bring light into the world. Were it not for this connection, the earth would be left in utter darkness ..

"The fact that unbelief prevails, that iniquity is increasing all around us, should not cause our faith to grow dim or our courage to waver.... If we will but seek God with all our hearts, if we will believe with that unyielding faith, the light of heaven will shine upon us, even as it shone upon the devoted Enoch."—*My Life Today, p. 8:1–2.*

"One of the most solemn and yet most glorious truths revealed in the Bible is that of Christ's Second Coming to complete the great work of redemption. To God's pilgrim people, so long left to sojourn in 'the region and shadow of death' a precious, joy-inspiring hope is given in the promise of His appearing, who is 'the resurrection and the life,' to 'bring home again His banished.' The doctrine of the Second Advent is the very keynote of Sacred Scriptures. From the day when the first pair turned their sorrowing steps from Eden, the children of faith have waited the coming of the Promised One to break the destroyer's power and bring them again to the lost Paradise. Holy men of old looked forward to the advent of the Messiah in glory, as the consummation of their hope. Enoch, only the seventh in descent from them that dwelt in Eden, he who for three centuries on earth walked with his God, was permitted to behold from afar the coming of the Deliverer. 'Behold,' he declared, 'the Lord cometh with ten thousands of His saints, to execute judgment upon all.' Jude 14–15. The patriarch Job in the night of his affliction exclaimed with unshaken trust: 'I know that my Redeemer liveth, and that He shall stand at the latter day upon the earth:...in my flesh shall I see God: whom I shall see for myself, and mine eyes shall behold, and not another.' Job 19:25–27."—*Great Controversy, p. 299:1.*

"Jude refers to the same period: 'The angels which kept not their first estate, but left their own habitation, He hath reserved in everlasting chains under darkness unto the judgment of the great day.' And, again, he quotes the words of Enoch: 'Behold, the Lord cometh with ten thousands of His saints, to execute judgment upon all.' Jude 6, 14–15. John declares that he 'saw the dead, small and great, stand before God; and the books were opened...and the dead were judged out of those things which were written in the books.' Revelation 20:12."—*Great Controversy, pp. 548:3–549:0.*

"The world was Enoch's field of labor. He had a message to an apostate world, words of warning and reproof for the sins that were flooding the world. In walking with God, Enoch was keeping a knowledge of God before the people. Although meek, and having a sense of his dependence upon God, his holy indignation waxed strong against those who were making void the law of God, and turning aside His counsels, putting in their place human counsels and human devising. He proclaimed the message: 'Behold, the Lord cometh with ten thousand of His saints, to execute judgment upon all, and to convince all that are ungodly among them of all their ungodly deeds which they have ungodly committed, and of all their hard speeches which ungodly sinners have spoken against them.' God had revealed the future to Enoch. The wonderful event of the Lord's coming was opened to his vision. 'He cometh with clouds, and every eye shall see Him.' This was present truth to Enoch, and was proclaimed by him to the world."—*Youth's Instructor, February 25, 1897, para. 4.*

"Enoch was a public teacher of the truth in the age in which he lived. He taught the truth; he lived the truth; and the character of the teacher who walked with God was in every way harmonious with the greatness and sacredness of his mission. Enoch was a prophet who spake as he was moved by the Holy Ghost. He was a light amid the moral darkness, a pattern man, a man who walked with God, being obedient to God's law,—that law which Satan had refused to obey, which Adam had transgressed, which Abel obeyed, and because of his obedience was murdered. And now God would demonstrate to the universe the falsity of Satan's charge that man cannot keep God's law. He would demonstrate that though man had sinned, he could so relate himself to God that he would have the mind and spirit of God and would be a representative symbol of Christ. This holy man was selected of God to denounce the wickedness of the world, and to evidence to the world that it is possible for man to keep all the law of God."—*Manuscript Releases, Vol. 6, p. 146:1.*

"Present the Word of God as the way in which a holy faith and a pure character may be attained. Offer a full and free salvation, not as coming from yourselves, but from Christ. Show your hearers their need of returning through repentance and faith to their loyalty; for all are on a level; all are condemned alike by that great moral standard of righteousness. Proclaim remission of sins through Christ, the only Sin-bearer, the only Sin-pardoner.

Proclaim the remission of sins through repentance toward God and faith in Christ, and God will ratify your testimony. With all assurance you can proclaim the means by which a holy character may be obtained as Enoch obtained it, through Christ Jesus." —*The Voice in Speech and Song, p. 340:1.*

"The Word of God includes the Scriptures of the Old Testament as well as of the New. One is not complete without the other. Christ declared that the truths of the Old Testament are as valuable as those of the New. Christ was as much man's Redeemer in the beginning of the world as He is today. Before He clothed His divinity with humanity and came to our world, the gospel massage was given by Adam, Seth, Enoch, Methuselah, and Noah. Abraham in Canaan and Lot in Sodom bore the message, and from generation to generation faithful messengers proclaimed the Coming One." —*Lift Him Up, p. 306:2.*

"The Lord is soon to come in the clouds of heaven, with power and great glory. Is there not enough in the truths which cluster around this event and in the preparation essential for it, to make us think solemnly of our duty? 'The Son of man shall come in His glory;...and before Him shall be gathered all nations.' This subject should be kept before the people as a means to an end,—that end the judgment, with its eternal punishments and rewards. Then God will render to every man according to his work. Enoch prophesied of these things, saying, 'Behold, the Lord cometh with ten thousands of His saints, to execute judgment upon all.' And Solomon, the preacher of righteousness, when making his declaration and appeal, presented the judgment to come. 'Let us hear the conclusion of the whole matter,' he said; 'Fear God, and keep His commandments; for this is the whole duty of man. For God shall bring every work into judgment, with every secret thing, whether it be good or whether it be evil.' " —*Review and Herald, June 18, 1901, para. 8*

"Because we do not know the exact hour of Christ's coming we are commanded to watch. 'Blessed are those servants, whom the Lord when he cometh shall find watching.' Those who watch for the Lord's return do not wait in idle expectancy. They purify their hearts by obedience to the truth. With vigilant watching they unite earnest working. Because they know that the Lord is at the door, their zeal is quickened to cooperate with divine intelligences in working for the salvation of souls. These are the faithful and wise servants, who give the Lord's household their portion of meat in due season. They are declaring the truth that is now especially applicable. As Enoch, Abraham, and Moses each declared the truth for his time, so will Christ's servants now give the special warning for their generation."—*Review and Herald, November 13, 1913, para. 4.*

"Like Enoch, we should earnestly proclaim the message of Christ's Second Coming. 'The day of the Lord,' the Scriptures declare, 'cometh as a thief in the night. For when they shall say, Peace and safety; then sudden destruction cometh upon them,…and they shall not escape.' In these words is emphasized the importance of being constantly prepared for this great event."—*Signs of the Times, October 12, 1904, para. 8.*

"God had other men to testify of Him in that day, though Enoch stood at the head. There was Noah, with his God-given message. And thus God's chosen representatives are traced from generation to generation, as they gave their message to the world, flashing the light of heaven upon the pathway of those who walk in darkness."—*Youth's Instructor, February 25, 1897, para. 5.*

Chapter 18
The Trials of Enoch

"The power of God that wrought with His servant was felt by those who heard. Some gave heed to the warning, and renounced their sins, but the multitudes mocked at the solemn message, and went on more boldly in their evil ways. The servants of God are to bear a similar message to the world in the last days, and it will also be received with unbelief and mockery. The antediluvian world rejected the warning words of him who walked with God. So will the last generation make light of the warnings of the Lord's messengers."—*Patriarchs and Prophets, p. 86:3.*

"How often those who trusted the Word of God, though in themselves utterly helpless, have stood the power of the whole world,—Enoch, pure in heart, holy in life, holding fast his faith in the triumph of righteousness against a corrupt and scoffing generation."—*Education, p. 254:2.*

"The men of that generation had mocked the folly of him who sought not to gather gold or silver, or to build up possessions here. But Enoch's heart was upon eternal treasures. He had looked upon the celestial city. He had seen the King in His glory in the midst of Zion. His mind, his heart, his conversation, were in heaven. The greater the existing iniquity, the more earnest was his longing for the home of God. While still on earth, he dwelt, by faith, in the realms of light."—*Patriarchs and Prophets, p. 87:2.*

"Christ is acquainted with all that is misunderstood and misrepresented by men. His children can afford to wait in calm patience and trust, no matter how much maligned and despised; for nothing is secret that shall not be made manifest, and those who honor God shall be honored by Him in the presence of men and angels.

" 'When men shall revile you, and persecute you,' said Jesus, 'rejoice and be exceeding glad.' And He pointed His hearers to the prophets who had spoken in the name of the Lord, as 'an example of suffering affliction, and of patience.' James 5:10. Abel, the very first Christian of Adam's children, died a martyr. Enoch walked with God, and the world knew Him not. Noah was mocked as a fanatic and an alarmist.... In every age God's chosen messengers have been reviled and persecuted, yet through their affliction, the knowledge of God has been spread abroad. Every disciple of Christ is to step into the ranks and carry forward the same work.... God means that truth shall be brought to the front and become the subject of examination and discussion, even through the contempt placed upon it. The minds of the people must be agitated."—*Mount of Blessing, pp. 32:3–33:2.*

"Not by their wealth, their education, or their position does God estimate men. He estimates them by their purity of motive and their beauty of character. He looks to see how much of His Spirit they possess, and how much of His likeness their life reveals. To be great in God's kingdom is to be as a little child in humility, in simplicity of faith, and in purity of love ..

"Of all the gifts that heaven can bestow upon men, fellowship with Christ in His sufferings is the most weighty trust and the highest honor. Not Enoch, who was translated to heaven, not Elijah, who ascended in a chariot of fire, was greater or more honored than John the Baptist, who perished alone in the dungeon. 'Unto you it is given in behalf of Christ, not only to believe on Him, but also to suffer for His sake.' "—*Ministry of Healing, pp. 477:5–478:2.*

"If you choose to throw off the sacred, restraining influence of the truth, Satan will lead you captive at his will. You will be in danger of giving scope to your appetites and passion, giving loose rein to lusts, to evil and abominable desires. Instead of bearing in your countenance a calm serenity under trial and affliction, like faithful Enoch, having your face radiant with hope and that peace which passeth understanding, you will stamp your countenance with carnal thoughts, with lustful desires. You will bear the impress of the satanic instead of the divine."—*2 Testimonies, p. 92:1.*

Chapter 19
The Question of Enoch

"Enoch walked with God three hundred years previously to his translation, and the state of the world was not more favorable for the perfection of Christian character than it is today. How did Enoch walk with God? He educated his mind and heart to ever feel the presence of God, and when in perplexity his prayers would ascend to God—to keep him, to teach him His will. 'What shall I do to honor thee my God?' was his prayer. His will was merged in the will of God, and his feet were constantly directed in the path of God's commandments. Enoch was a representative of those who shall be on the earth when Christ shall come, who will be translated to Heaven and never see death. It is fitting that we pray, as did David, 'Open thou mine eyes, that I may behold wondrous things out of Thy law.' "—*Signs of the Times, December 29, 1887, para. 11.*

"God must be ever in our thoughts. We must hold converse with Him while we walk by the way, and while our hands are engaged in labor. In all the purposes and pursuits of life we must inquire, What will the Lord have me to do? How shall I please Him who has given His life a ransom for me? Thus may we walk with God, as did Enoch of old; and ours may be the testimony which he received, that he pleased God."—*Our High Calling, p. 61:5.*

"Joseph preserved his integrity when surrounded by idolaters in Egypt, in the midst of sin and blasphemy and corrupting influences. When tempted to turn from the path of virtue, his answer was, 'How can I do this great wickedness, and sin against God?' Gen 39:9. Enoch, Joseph and Daniel depended upon a strength that was infinite. This is the only course of safety for Christians to pursue in our day."—*Our High Calling, p. 278:4.*

" 'Every man's work shall be made manifest; for the day shall declare it, because it shall be revealed by fire; and the fire shall try every man's work of what sort it is. If any man's work abide which he hath built thereupon, he shall receive a reward.' Why, then, do not men exercise themselves unto godliness? Why do they bear thorn berries? it is because they are not grafted into the tame olive tree. They are not converted. Their works testify of them that they do not abide in Christ. They do not, as is represented by Christ, eat His flesh and drink His blood. If they did, they would through faith have a vital connection with Christ, and work the works of God. The character is transformed, not by a slight change in some customs and practices, but by a work divine; for the Lord says, 'A new heart will I give thee.' This is a death to self and sin, and a new life altogether. 'I live,' said Paul; 'yet not I, but Christ liveth in me.' Has the dry branch been grafted into the living vine stock? Then has the graft taken connection with the vine fiber by fiber? Is it one with the parent stock? If it is, then will it bear the fruit of the vine. If we are one with Christ, we shall be Christlike. This is the great power of God. And yet we are commanded: 'Work out your own salvation with fear and trembling. For it is God which worketh in you both to will and to do of His good pleasure.' The great privileges of the Christian have been opened before us. He who daily depends upon Christ will work out Christ in spirit, in words, in actions. He may be compelled to rebuke sin, to reprove, to exhort, to rebuke with all long-suffering and doctrine. On special occasions his spirit may be stirred within him to expose sin and wickedness; but in it all he has the Spirit of Christ. It is a work that must be done. We may live a life of close connection with Jesus, of oneness with Christ. The mind should be kept in a prayerful frame, looking to Jesus moment by moment, asking at every step, 'Is this the way of the Lord?' This is the way Enoch walked with God. We are to be learners of one another and doers of the Word of God."—*Signs of the Times, September 26, 1892, para. 5.*

Chapter 20
The Translation of Enoch

"In the midst of a life of active labor, Enoch steadfastly maintained his communion with God. The greater and more pressing his labors, the more constant and earnest were his prayers. He continued to exclude himself, at certain periods, from all society. After remaining for a time among the people, laboring to benefit them by instruction and example, he would withdraw, to spend a season in solitude, hungering and thirsting for that divine knowledge which God alone can impart. Communing thus with God, Enoch came more and more to reflect the divine image. His face was radiant with a holy light, even the light that shineth in the face of Jesus. As he came forth from these divine communings, even the ungodly beheld with awe the impress of heaven upon his countenance."—*Patriarchs and Prophets, pp. 86:4–87:0.*

"Enoch continued to grow more heavenly while communing with God. His face was radiant with a holy light which would remain upon his countenance while instructing those who would hear his words of wisdom. His heavenly and dignified appearance struck the people with awe. The Lord loved Enoch because he steadfastly followed Him and abhorred iniquity and earnestly sought heavenly knowledge, that he might do His will perfectly. He yearned to unite himself more closely to God, whom he feared, reverenced, and adored.

"God would not permit Enoch to die as other men, but sent His angels to take him to heaven without seeing death. In the presence of the righteous and the wicked, Enoch was removed from them. Those who loved him thought that God might have left him in some of his places of retirement, but after seeking him diligently, and being unable to find him, reported that he was not, for God took him."—*Story of Redemption, p. 59:2.*

" 'Blessed are the pure in heart, for they shall see God.' (Matthew 5:8). For three hundred years Enoch had been seeking purity of soul, that he might be in harmony with Heaven. For three centuries he had walked with God. Day by day he had longed for a closer union, nearer and nearer had grown the communion, until God took him to Himself. He had stood at the threshold of the eternal world, only a step between him and the land of the blest,—and now the portals opened, the walk with God, so long pursued on earth continued, and he passed through the gates of the Holy City—the first from among men to enter there.

"His loss was felt on earth. The voice that had been heard day after day in warning and instruction was missed. There were some, both of the righteous and the wicked, who had witnessed his departure. And hoping that he might have been conveyed to some one of his places of retirement, those who loved him made diligent search, as afterward the sons of the prophets searched for Elijah, but without avail. They reported that he was not, for God had taken him."—*Patriarchs and Prophets, p. 87:3–88:1.*

"The Lord here teaches a lesson of importance by the translation of Enoch, a descendant of fallen Adam, that all would be rewarded, who by faith would rely upon the promised Sacrifice and faithfully obey His commandments. Two classes are here again represented which were to exist until the second coming of Christ—the righteous and the wicked, the rebellious and the loyal. God will remember the righteous, who fear Him. On account of His dear Son He will respect and honor them and give them everlasting life. But the wicked, who trample upon His authority, He will cut off and destroy from the earth, and they will be as though they had not been."—*Story of Redemption, pp. 59:3–60:0.*

"By the translation of Enoch the Lord designed to teach an important lesson. There was danger that men would yield to discouragement, because of the fearful results of Adam's sin. Many were ready to exclaim, 'What profit is it that we have feared the Lord and have kept His ordinances, since a heavy curse is resting upon the race, and death is the portion of us all?' But the instructions which God gave to Adam, and which were repeated by Seth, and exemplified by Enoch, swept away the gloom and darkness, and gave hope to man, that as through Adam came death, so through the promised Redeemer would come life and immortality. Satan was urging upon men the belief that there was no reward for the righteous or punishment for the wicked, and that it was impossible for men to obey the divine statutes.

"But in the case of Enoch, God declares 'that He is, and that He is a rewarder of them that diligently seek Him.' Hebrews 11:6. He shows what He will do for those who keep His commandments. Men were taught that it is possible to obey the Law of God,—that even while living in the midst of the sinful and corrupt, they were able, by the grace of God, to resist temptation, and become pure and holy. They saw in his example the blessedness of such a life, and his translation was an evidence of the truth of His prophecy concerning the hereafter, with its award of joy and glory and immortal life to the obedient, and of condemnation, woe, and death to the transgressor."—*Patriarchs and Prophets, p. 88:2.*

"In the case of Enoch the desponding faithful were taught that, although living among a corrupt and sinful people, who were in open and daring rebellion against God, their Creator, yet if they would obey Him and have faith in the promised Redeemer, they could work righteousness like the faithful Enoch, be accepted of God, and finally exalted to His heavenly throne."—*Story of Redemption, p. 60:2.*

"By faith Enoch 'was translated that he should not see death; .. for before his translation he had this testimony, that he pleased God.' Hebrews 11:5. In the midst of a world by its iniquity doomed to destruction, Enoch lived a life of such close communion with God that he was not permitted to fall under the power of death. The godly character of this prophet represents the state of holiness which must be attained by those who shall be 'redeemed from the earth' (Revelation 14:3) at the time of Christ's second advent. Then, as in the world before the Flood, iniquity will prevail. Following the promptings of their corrupt hearts and the teachings of a deceptive philosophy, men will rebel against the authority of Heaven. But like Enoch, God's people will seek for purity of heart and conformity to His will, until they shall reflect the likeness of Christ. Like Enoch, they will warn the world of the Lord's second coming and of the judgments to be visited upon transgression, and by their holy conversation and example they will condemn the sins of the ungodly. As Enoch was translated to heaven before the destruction of the world by water, so the living righteous will be translated from the earth before the destruction by fire."—*Patriarchs and Prophets, pp. 88:3–89:0.*

"Enoch, separating himself from the world, and spending much of his time in prayer and in communion with God, represents God's loyal people in the last days, who will be separate from the world. Unrighteousness will prevail to a dreadful extent upon the earth. Men will give themselves up to follow every imagination of their corrupt hearts and carry out their deceptive philosophy and rebel against the authority of high heaven.

"God's people will separate themselves from the unrighteous practices of those around them and will seek for purity of thought and holy conformity to His will until His divine image will be reflected in them. Like Enoch, they will be fitting for translation to heaven. While they endeavor to instruct and warn the world, they will not conform to the spirit and customs of unbelievers but will condemn them by their holy conversation and godly example. Enoch's translation to heaven just before the destruction of the world by a flood represents the translation of all the living righteous from the earth previous to its destruction by fire. The saints will be glorified in the presence of those who have hated them for their loyal obedience to God's righteous commandments." —*Story of Redemption, p. 61:1.*

"The Lord gave me a view of other worlds. Wings were given me, and an angel attended me from the city to a place that was bright and glorious…. The inhabitants of the place were…noble, majestic, and lovely. They bore the express image of Jesus, and their countenances beamed with holy joy, expressive of the freedom and happiness of the place. I asked one of them why they were so much more lovely than those on the earth. The reply was, 'We have lived in strict obedience to the commandments of God, and have not fallen by disobedience, like those on earth'…. Then I was taken to a world which had twelve moons. There I saw good old Enoch, who had been translated…. I asked him if this was the place he was taken to from the earth. He said, 'It is not. The city is my home, and I have come to visit this place.' He moved about the place as if perfectly at home…. Then the angel said, 'You must go back, and if you are faithful, you, with the 144,000, shall have the privilege of visiting all the worlds and viewing the handiwork of God.' "—*Early Writings, pp. 39:3–40:0.*

"We can have what Enoch had. We can have Christ as our constant Companion. Enoch walked with God, and when assailed by the tempter, he could talk with God about it. He had no 'It is written' as we have, but he had a knowledge of his heavenly Companion. He made God his Counselor, and was closely bound up with Jesus. And Enoch was honored in his course. He was translated to heaven without seeing death. And those who will be translated at the close of time, will ever be representing Him in all their life-practices. Selfishness will be cut out by the roots." —*Manuscript 38, 1897.*

"Be ambitious for the Master's glory, to cultivate every grace of character. In every phrase of your character building you are to please God. This you may do: for Enoch pleased Him though living in a degenerate age. And there are Enochs living in our day…[Jesus] says 'Without Me ye can do nothing.' John 15:5. Remember this. If you have made mistakes, you certainly gain a victory if you see these mistakes and regard them as beacons of warning. Thus you turn defeat into victory, disappointing the enemy and honoring your Redeemer.

"A character formed according to the divine likeness is the only treasure that we can take from this world to the next. Those who are under the instruction of Christ in this world will take every divine attainment with them to the heavenly mansions."—*Christ Object Lessons, p. 332:1–2.*

" 'By faith Enoch was translated that he should not see death; .. for before his translation he had this testimony, that he pleased God.'

"To such a communion God is calling us. As was Enoch's, so must be their holiness of character who shall be redeemed from among men at the Lord's second coming."—*8 Testimonies, p. 331:2–3.*

"With the Word of God in his hands, every human being, wherever his lot in life may be cast, may have such companionship as he shall choose. In its pages he may hold converse with the noblest and best of the human race, and may listen to the voice of the Eternal as He speaks with men. As he studies and meditates upon the themes into which 'the angels desire to look,' he may have their companionship. He may follow the steps of the heavenly Teacher, and listen to his words as when He taught on mountain and plain and sea. He may dwell in this world in the atmosphere of heaven, imparting to earth's sorrowing and tempted ones thoughts of hope and longings for holiness; himself coming closer and still closer into fellowship with the Unseen; like him of old who walked with God, drawing nearer and nearer the threshold of the eternal world, until the portals shall open, and he shall enter there. He will find himself no stranger. The voices that will greet him are the voices of the holy ones, who, unseen, were on earth his companions,—voices that here he learned to distinguish and to love. He who through the Word of God has lived in fellowship with heaven, will find himself at home in heaven's companionship."—*Education, p. 127:1.*

"The Lord would not permit Enoch to die like other men, but sent His angels to take him to Heaven without seeing death. In the presence of the righteous and the wicked, Enoch was removed from them. Those who loved him thought that God might have left him in some of his places of retirement; but after seeking diligently, and being unable to find him, they reported that he was not, for God took him."—*Signs of the Times, February 20, 1879, para. 7.*

"[Jude 14–15]. The sermon preached by Enoch, and his translation to heaven was a convincing argument to all living in Enoch's time. It was an argument that Methuselah and Noah could use with power to show that the righteous could be translated (*MS 46, 1895*)."—*S.D.A. Bible Commentary, Vol. 1, p. 1088/2:5.*

"God's people will separate themselves from the unrighteous practices of those around them, and will seek for purity of thought, and holy conformity to His will, until His divine image will be reflected in them. Like Enoch they will be fitting for translation to Heaven. While they endeavor to instruct and warn the world, they will not conform to the spirit and customs of unbelievers, but will condemn them by their holy conversation and godly example. Enoch's translation to Heaven just before the destruction of the world by a flood, represents the translation of all the living righteous from the earth previous to its destruction by fire. The saints will be glorified in the presence of these who have hated them for their loyal obedience to God's righteous commandments."—*Spirit of Prophecy, Vol. 1, p. 65:1.*

"Enoch represents those who shall remain upon the earth and be translated to Heaven without seeing death. He represents that company that are to live amid the perils of the last days, and withstand all the corruption, vileness, sin, and iniquity, and yet be unsullied by it all. We can stand as did Enoch. There has been provision made for us. Help has been laid upon One that is mighty; and we all can take hold upon His mighty strength. Angels of God, that excel in strength, are sent to minister to those who shall be heirs of salvation. These angels, when they see that we are doing the very utmost on our part to be overcomers, will do their part, and their light will shine around about us, and sway back the influence of the evil angels that are around us, and will make a fortification around us as a wall of fire. Ample provisions have been made for us when we are burdened, and weary, and cast down, and in distress."—*Review and Herald, April 19, 1870, para. 11.*

"In the destruction of the inhabitants of the old world by the flood is clearly represented the faith of all those who continue to transgress the law of God. Enoch's translation to Heaven represents the commandment-keeping people of God who will be alive upon the earth when Christ shall come the second time, and who will be glorified in the sight of those who hated them because they would keep the commandments of God. These also will be translated to Heaven without seeing death, as Enoch and Elijah were."—*Review and Herald, April 29, 1875, para. 8.*

"Now Enoch was a representative of those who will be upon the earth when Christ shall come, who will be translated to heaven without seeing death."—*Last Day Events, p. 71:3.*

"Brother P's ideas of order and organization have been in direct opposition to God's plan of order. There is order in heaven, and it is to be imitated by those upon earth who are heirs of salvation. The nearer mortals attain to the order and arrangement of heaven, the nearer are they brought to that acceptable state before God which will make them subjects of the heavenly kingdom and give them that fitness for translation from earth to heaven which Enoch possessed preparatory to his translation."—*2 Testimonies, p. 697:3–698:0.*

"Were Enoch upon the earth today, his heart would be in harmony with all God's requirements; he would walk with God, although surrounded with influences which are the most wicked and debasing. So may we remain pure and uncorrupted. He was a representative of the saints who live amid the perils and corruptions of the last days. For his faithful obedience to God, he was translated. So, also, the faithful, who are alive and remain, will be translated. They will be removed from a sinful and corrupt world to the pure joys of heaven."—*Review and Herald, April 15, 1909, para. 8.*

" 'Enoch walked with God; and he was not; for God took him.' And when God takes the members of His church to heaven, it will be because they have walked with Him here on this earth, receiving from above strength and wisdom which enables them to serve Him aright. Those who are taken to God will be men and women who now pray in humility and contrition, whose hearts are not lifted in vanity. In their dealing with their fellowmen they represent Christ. Those who dishonor God while professing to serve Him, are one with the world. In the last great day they will be found among the number who knew their Lord's will, but did it not."—*Signs of the Times, June 19, 1901, para. 9.*

"Will you have eternal life? If so, you must turn away from the pleasure of the world. The wickedness in this age is as great as it was in the days of Noah. But one man was found that walked with God even in that crooked and perverse generation. Enoch kept his mind stayed upon God, and God did not leave him but finally took him from this sinful world. This man was a representative of those who will be translated to heaven when Christ comes to gather His people. Are we ready for the appearing of Christ? Have we washed our robes and made them clean in the blood of the Lamb?" —*Manuscript Releases, Vol. 3, p. 75:1.*

Chapter 21
The Significance of Enoch

"Family religion, family holiness, is now to be honored as never before. If ever a people needed to walk before God as did Enoch, Seventh-day Adventists need to do so now, showing their sincerity by pure words, full of sympathy, tenderness, and love.

"There are times when words of reproof and rebuke are called for. Those who are out of the right way must be aroused to see their peril. A message must be given that shall startle them from the lethargy which enchains their senses."—7 *Testimonies, p. 155:2.*

"We are living in an evil age. The perils of the last days thicken around us. Because iniquity abounds, the love of many waxes cold. Enoch walked with God three hundred years. Now the shortness of time seems to be urged as a motive to seek righteousness. Should it be necessary that the terrors of the day of God be held before us in order to compel us to right action? Enoch's case is before us. Hundreds of years he walked with God. He lived in a corrupt age, when moral pollution was teeming all around him; yet he trained his mind to run in this channel, and he bore the impress of the divine. His countenance was lighted up with the light which shineth in the face of Jesus. Enoch had temptations as well as we. He was surrounded with society no more friendly to righteousness than is that which surrounds us. The atmosphere he breathed was tainted with sin and corruption, the same as ours; yet he lived a life of holiness. He was unsullied with the prevailing sins of the age in which he lived. So may we remain pure and uncorrupted. He was a representative of the saints who live amid the perils and corruptions of the last days. For his faithful obedience to God he was translated. So, also, the faithful, who are alive and remain, will be translated. They will be removed from a sinful and corrupt world to the pure joys of heaven.

" 'The course of God's people should be upward and onward to victory. A greater than Joshua is leading the armies of Israel…' 'Lo, I am with you always, even to the end of the world.' 'Be of good cheer, I have overcome the world.' He will lead us on to certain victory. What God promises, He is able at any time to perform. And the work He gives His people to do, He is able to accomplish by them. If we live a life of perfect obedience, His promises will be fulfilled toward us."—*2 Testimonies, pp. 121:1–122:1.*

"The fact that unbelief prevails, that iniquity is increasing all around us, should not cause our faith to grow dim, nor our courage to waver. How was it with Enoch in his day? Was a life of holiness more easy than it is now? Was the world more favorable to a growth in grace? Was the earth less corrupt, when God was forced to destroy its inhabitants for their heaven-defying wickedness? If we will but seek God with all our hearts, if we will work with that same determined zeal, and believe with that unyielding faith, the light of heaven will shine upon us, even as it shone upon the devoted Enoch."—*Review and Herald, October 23, 1888, para. 11.*

"Our great need today is for men who are baptized with the Holy Spirit of God—men who walk with God as did Enoch. We do not want men who are so narrow in their outlook that they will circumscribe the work instead of enlarging it, or who follow the motto: 'Religion is religion; business is business.' We need men who are farseeing, who can take in the situation and reason from cause to effect."—*The Publishing Ministry, pp. 63:3–64:0.*

"Enoch, the seventh from Adam, was ever prophesying the coming of the Lord. This great event had been revealed to him in vision. Abel, though dead, is ever speaking of the blood of Christ which alone can make our offerings and gifts perfect. The Bible has accumulated and bound up together its treasures for this last generation. All the great events and solemn transactions of Old Testament history have been, and are, repeating themselves in the church in these last days. There is Moses still speaking, teaching self-renunciation by wishing himself blotted from the Book of life for his fellow men, that they might be saved. David is leading the intercession of the church for the salvation of souls to the ends of the earth. The prophets are still testifying of the sufferings of

Christ and the glory that should follow. There the whole accumulated truths are presented in force to us that we may profit by their teachings. We are under the influence of the whole. What manner of persons ought we to be to whom all this rich light of inheritance has been given. Concentrating all the influence of the past with new increased light of the present, accrued power is given to all who will follow the light. Their faith will increase, and be brought into exercise at the present time, awakening an energy and an intensely increased earnestness, and through dependence upon God for His power to replenish the world and send the light of the Sun of Righteousness to the ends of the earth."—*3 Selected Messages, p. 339:1.*

Conclusion

"He that is to come says, 'Behold, I come quickly; and my reward is with Me, to give every man according as his work shall be.' Every good deed done by the people of God as the fruit of their faith, will have its corresponding reward. As one star differeth from another star in glory, so will believers have its corresponding reward. As one star differeth from another star in glory, so will believers have their different spheres assigned them in the future life. Will the man who did not walk with God as did Enoch, but who walked by the side of Satan, listening to his suggestions, obeying his promptings, imperiling his own soul and the souls for whom Christ died, to gratify the carnal mind, giving lenity to sin in his example—will such a man be found among the overcomers?"—*Testimonies to Ministers, pp. 428:3–429:0.*

"It is our privilege to carry with us the credentials of our faith,—love, joy, and peace. When we do this, we shall be able to present the mighty arguments of the cross of Christ. When we learn to walk by faith and not by feeling, we shall have help from God just when we need it, and His peace will come into our hearts. It was this simple life of obedience and trust that Enoch lived. If we learn this lesson of simple trust, ours may be the testimony that he received, that he pleased God. Then instead of mourning and bitter repining, we shall make melody in our hearts to the Lord. 'In the world,' says Christ, 'ye shall have tribulation; but be of good cheer; I have overcome the world.' "—*Historical Sketches of the Foreign Missions of the Seventh-day Adventists, p. 133:1.*

"God sees every heart and knows the excuses suggested by Satan by which he seeks to ensnare every soul. He fully appreciates our danger, while we do not. He is not willing that any should perish in sin; but that all should repent and live. Hence, the oft repeated plea that we should not be deceived and lost. There is one thing however, which infinite love cannot do; it cannot requite the unrepentant wicked. What is it to be in an unsaved condition? Is it not to be living without that full confidence in God which is born of love, which leads us to take Him at His word? Believing His promises, we walk with Him and talk with Him as did Enoch and Elijah and the faithful of all the ages past. They were called pilgrims and strangers in the earth, because they had so much faith in God that they would follow His instruction so completely that they became very different from the world in their plans, and their objectives in life were also different."—*Bible Training School, November 1, 1911, para. 1.*

"Enoch walked with God 300 years, and we can walk with God from day to day. He had in his heart the living principles of the law of God, and the Holy Spirit rested upon him. He looked forward to the coming of Christ, and prophesied of the appearing of our Lord that is now so near at hand. If we believe that Christ is soon coming, we shall talk of our hope. Jesus said, 'Let not your heart be troubled: ye believe in God, believe also in Me. In My Father's house are many mansions: if it were not so, I would have told you. I go to prepare a place for you. And if I go and prepare a place for you, I will come again, and receive you unto myself; that where I am, there ye may be also.' Christ has warned us to watch and pray that we may be ready for His coming; and shall we not watch and be patient? Shall we be deceived by the powers of darkness? May God help us that our lamps may be found trimmed and burning!"—*Review and Herald, April 21, 1891, para. 7.*

"The church today needs men who, like Enoch, walk with God, revealing Christ to the World. Church members need to reach a higher standard. Heavenly messengers are waiting to communicate with those who have sunk self out of sight, whose lives are a fulfilling of the words, 'I live; yet not I, but Christ liveth in me: and the life which I now live in the flesh I live by the faith of the Son of God, who loved me, and gave himself for me.' Of such men and women must the church be composed before her light can shine forth to the world in clear, distinct rays. Our view of the Sun of Righteousness are clouded by self-seeking. Christ is crucified afresh by many who through self-indulgence allow Satan to gain control over them. The church needs men of devotion to bear to the world the message of salvation, pointing sinners to the

Lamb of God, men who, by their works of righteousness and their pure, true words, can lift their fellow men out of the pit of degradation."—*Review and Herald, December 4, 1900, para. 12.*

"Those who profess the religion of Christ should understand the responsibility resting upon them. They should feel that this is an individual walk. If each would realize this, and would act accordingly, the church would be as mighty as an army with banners. The heavenly Dove would hover over us, and the light of the glory of God would no more be shut away from us than it was from the devoted Enoch."—*The Watchman, March 10, 1908, para. 3.*

"Every faculty that we possess has been provided for us in Christ; for when God gave His Son to our world, He included all heaven in His gift. And God would have men value their powers as a sacred gift from Him. A spark of God's own life has been breathed into the human body, making man a living soul, the possessor of moral endowments, and a will to direct his own course of action. He has the privilege of becoming a partaker of the divine nature. This will give him power to conquer evil, and love and choose that which is good. He has a conscience, which, under the control of God, will approve the right and condemn the wrong. And he may, if he will, have fellowship with God. He may walk and talk with God as did Enoch. This holy companionship is denied to none who will believe on Christ as their personal Saviour."—*Signs of the Times, August 26, 1897, para. 8.*

" 'Be ye therefore perfect, even as your Father which is in heaven is perfect.' 'Do all things without murmurings and disputings; that ye may be blameless and harmless, the sons of God, without rebuke, in the midst of a crooked and perverse nation, among whom ye shine as lights in the world; holding forth the word of life; that I may rejoice in the day of Christ, that I have not run in vain, neither labored in vain.' The Lord appeared unto Abraham, and said, 'Walk before me, and be thou perfect.' Enoch walked with God three hundred years. 'Epaphras, who is one of you, a servant of Christ, saluteth you, always laboring fervently for you in prayers, that ye may stand perfect and complete in all the will of God.' 'Christ in you, the hope of glory: whom we preach, warning every man, and teaching every man in all wisdom; that we may present every man perfect in Christ Jesus: where unto I also labor, striving according to His working, which worketh in me mightily.' "—*Youth's Instructor, August 31, 1893, para. 1.*

"God permits men to pass under the fire of temptation that they may see if there is alloy in their characters; for they cannot inherit their heirship to the eternal crown unless they are tested and proved by the Lord. Take time to watch and pray, to assure yourselves that you have the presence of Jesus, and can counsel with Him in regard to the work He has given into your hands, as did Enoch of old. You who occupy important positions of responsibility, how much you need Jesus, how much you need to watch and pray that you may be fervent in spirit, serving the Lord. Will you gather business to your soul, and leave Christ out on the plea that you have not time to commune with Him? Why violate conscience? Why put such confidence in your own strength?" —*Manuscript Releases, Vol. One, p. 97:2.*

"The time has now come when we need to hide in the cleft of the Rock, and view the character of God. Enoch walked with God 300 years. He reflected upon God, he contemplated his character, and his life was well-pleasing in the sight of God. And on the part of His children today there should be just such a meditation upon the Word of God. It should not only be read, but carefully studied; for it furnishes the only safe standard and guide in the formation of moral character, and the only sure road to intellectual culture. (*MS 29, 1896, pp. 6, 8, October 31, 1896*)."—*Manuscript Releases, Vol. Four, pp. 411:4–412:0.*

"Human knowledge, human philosophy, cannot transform character. But the Lord can take fallen man, and by grace transform him. He says, 'I will make a man more precious than fine gold; even a man than the golden wedge of Ophir—fitted, like Enoch, to walk with God, to be the companion of angels. In Christianity there is a wonder-working power."—*Manuscript Releases, Vol. Eighteen, p. 334:1.*

"We fight not against flesh and blood, but against principalities, and powers, and spiritual wickedness in high places, and God is with us. We are not to consider that the smartness of men will bring success. One may have all the learning possible for a human being to comprehend, and yet he may be alone, and without Christ he can do nothing. Do you walk humbly before Him? Have you a cherishing of inward sins, heart burnings against any? Are you seeking God with all your heart? Now, we can bear to be separated from everything else but the Spirit of God. We want the inspiration of the cross, making us to fall helpless, and the Lord will lift us up. Christ prayed not that His followers should be taken out of the world, but that they might be kept from the evil that is in the world. We can go through the world as did Enoch. The world was then no more favorable for the formation of Christian character than it is in our time."—*Sermons and Talks, Vol. Two, p. 96:6.*

"We are too much inclined to be influenced by words of men, and not depend wholly upon God and have faith in God. Unless these men will walk with God as did Enoch, they will fall."—*The Ellen G. White 1888 Materials, pp. 465:3–466:0.*

"Enoch walked with God, and he was not, for God took him. The Lord would have us walk with Him. If He directs the work, it will move in His way, and will bear His impress."—*The Ellen G. White Materials, p. 1321:2.*

"And Enoch lived sixty and five years, and begat Methuselah:

"And Enoch walked with God after he begat Methuselah three hundred years, and begat sons and daughters.

"And all the days of Enoch were three hundred sixty and five years:

"And Enoch walked with God: and he was not; for God took him."—*Genesis 5:21–24.*

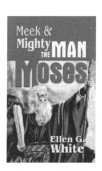

Meek and Mighty The Man Moses

A compilation of Ellen G. White's writings on the life of Moses from *The Signs of the Times* and *Patriarchs and Prophets*.

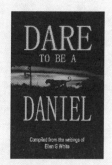

Dare to be a Daniel

A compilation of Ellen G. White's writings from *The Youth's Instructor* and other sources on the life of Daniel.

Other Titles from TEACH Services, Inc.

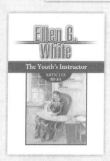

The Youth's Instructor Articles

A compilation of about 470 of Ellen G. White's articles that were originally published (1852–1914) in magazine form. Facsimile.

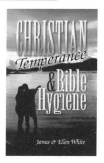

Christian Temperance & Bible Hygiene

This collection of writings by James and Ellen G. White will both inspire and instruct you in temperance and hygiene from a Biblical point of view.

We'd love to have you download our catalog of titles we publish at:

www.TEACHServices.com

or write or email us your thoughts, reactions, or criticism about this or any other book we publish at:

TEACH Services, Inc.
254 Donovan Road
Brushton, NY 12916

info@TEACHServices.com

or you may call us at:

518/358-3494

Produced in partnership with
LNFBooks.com